ENDORSEMENTS

"Given the success of this performance and its impact on our community of patients, survivors and providers, SMIL hopes to continue our support of the mission of 'A 2nd Act' through future collaborations."

John Freeman, Director of Sales & Marketing
Scottsdale Medical Imaging

"What an inspiration these women are to others struggling with cancer, being able to take a tragedy/hardship in life and see the blessings from it. Remarkable women making a difference in this world!"

Kelly B. Huey MSW, LCSW, OSW-C
Director of Integrative Services & Social Work
Ironwood Cancer & Research Centers

"The grace, humor and strength with which these women face their personal battles with cancer should serve to inspire and enlighten anyone facing a similar battle."

Jim Brewer
Executive Director
Arizona Chapter, The Leukemia & Lymphoma Society

presents:

SURVIVORS TAKE A REAL STAGE

CANCER SURVIVORS CHANGING THE QUESTION FROM "**WHY ME?**" TO "**WHAT NEXT?**"

A2ndAct.org

A 2nd Act presents:

Cancer Survivors Changing the Question
from "Why Me?" to "What Next?"

Cover design and book layout by
La Verne Abe Harris

ISBN-13: 978-1985107687

To order additional copies,
or to buy books in quantity, please visit
www.A2ndAct.org

DEDICATION

If you're going through hell, keep going.
-Winston Churchill

As anyone who's ever had cancer, or watched some-one battle cancer, can attest to, the disease is exactly the kind of hell dear Winston had in mind. The key is to keep going. That's true whether it refers to treat-ment or life in general. And neither of those are solo journeys.

This book, then, is dedicated to the women whose stories lie within; the brave women who created 2nd Acts. It's also dedicated to the millions of cancer sur-vivors and their loved ones who might be touched by their words.

Lastly, this book is dedicated to all of the sponsors, donors, and grantors who, through their generosity, have allowed us to bring these survivors' stories to stage and share them with others.

TABLE OF CONTENTS

INTRODUCTION

Any woman cancer survivor can tell you precisely where she was the moment she heard the words that changed her life forever: "You have cancer." A tsunami of doctors and drugs, procedures and scans, hurry up and wait ensue. Then, after months, maybe years, the waters of frenetic activity part. The big day arrives. Treatment is over.

But wait! There was safety and structure in that treatment. As survivors, we are suddenly struck by the realization there is no Humpty Dumpty moment when all the pieces of our lives will be put back together, rebuilding the person we once were. Rather, we often find ourselves still dragging the carcass of our illness behind us. Whether we're told we have no evidence of disease, or that we must live with our cancer, what will fill the holes now that the diagnosis and treatment stages have leveled off? How do we push "play" on a once-paused life? What was it all for?

I know this first hand, as do the more than 8 million women survivors of all cancers in America. The cancer journey will forever be a part of our story. It is a story in two acts. Act I was our life before cancer. Now our 2nd Act must begin.

I'm a writer by profession, and my non-fiction work makes me a researcher as well. I stumbled on statistics supporting the idea that "healing is helping" while working on a book in my pre-cancer days. When I came across that same volunteering research as my post-cancer self, I realized that this most important element of healing – giving to others in some way, any way – was missing from the checklist of other support organizations.

Furthermore, whether aware of that research or not, women survivors across the country are taking their lives back by doing amazing things in their 2nd Acts. They're using their newly realized gifts of life and experience to give back to the greater good. They're making sense of their cancer journey and finding its purpose in their lives. I've had the honor of meeting hundreds of them face to face. And that's when my brain's lightbulb switched to the "on" position - and A2ndAct.org was born!

A2ndAct.org supports and celebrates these women survivors by giving them a platform from which to share their stories, our newly rebranded performances : "S.T.A.R.S!: Survivors Take A Real Stage." These curated stage performances feature 8 women survivors of ALL cancers, local to their performance city, using the centuries old craft of storytelling. They are ordinary women inspiring their audiences to create their own 2nd Acts, regardless of what life challenge might lie before them.

The money raised from these performances (and the purchase of this book, and other fundraisers) allows us to make micro-grants to women survivors, ready to reenter their lives and begin or grow their 2nd Acts. Most importantly, the money stays in the cites where it was raised.

Within the pages of this book, you'll find the amazing stories of the women who have graced our stage, along with our hope that you, too, will be inspired to overcome whatever obstacle might be blocking your path. We further hope that you'll share what you learn with others who might also need to create a 2nd Act.

As performances occur, we'll add those cast members' stories in new editions of this book. The beauty of the printed word is that, whether one lives in a performance city or not, the opportunity for inspiration is just fingertips away.

I thank you for your support, as woman by woman, city by city, we change survivors' life focus from "why me?" to "what next!"

Judy Pearson
Cancer Survivor and Founder
A2ndAct.org

AMERICAN WOMEN AND CANCER

An estimated **843,820** women in the United States will be diagnosed with some form of cancer in 2016. There are nearly **8 MILLION** women survivors in the US.

That's a number greater than the population of New Zealand, Hong Kong, or Norway.

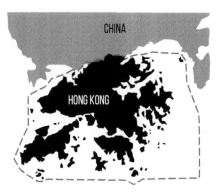

It's also greater than the **combined** populations of Luxembourg (bordered by Belgium, Germany and France), Jamaica and Puerto Rico.

1:3

One in three women will be diagnosed with some form of cancer during their lifetime. If not you, you will know her. She may be your friend, neighbor, mother, sister or even your daughter.

La Verne Abe Harris

Sources: American Cancer Society Statistics 2016, Wikipedia

A 2ND ACT: INTRODUCTION

Cancer doesn't end when treatment does.
Even if the disease is cured tomorrow,
women survivors would still face challenges
they never expected:

CANCER'S COLLATERAL DAMAGE
Financial Toxicity, Careers, Relationships, and Fear

FINANCIAL TOXICITY

Cancer survivors file for bankruptcy **2.5 TIMES** more often than the rest of the population. Fred Hutchinson Cancer Research Center coined the phrase "financial toxicity" of cancer.

CAREERS

30% of women cancer survivors in a University of Michigan study say they have had difficulty returning to their careers.

RELATIONSHIPS

Men are **7 TIMES** more likely than women to end a relationship due to significant illness.

FEAR

70% of women survivors fear a recurrence of their cancer.

La Verne Abe Harris

Sources: Fred Hutchinson Cancer Research Center, University of Michigan, Huntsman Cancer Institute

ECONOMY

Women account for **75% - 85%** of all consumer purchases.

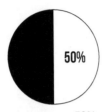

Women hold up **50%** of the economic sky in America.

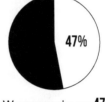

Women make up **47%** of labor force.

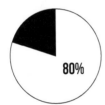

Women make approximately **80%** of health care decisions for their families and are more likely to be the caregivers when a family member falls ill.

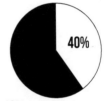

40% of all households with children under the age of 18 include mothers who are either the sole or primary source of income for the family.

La Verne Abe Harris

Sources: Pew Research Center Data, 2013; U.S. Department of Labor, 2013; Boston Consulting Group, Nielson, and others

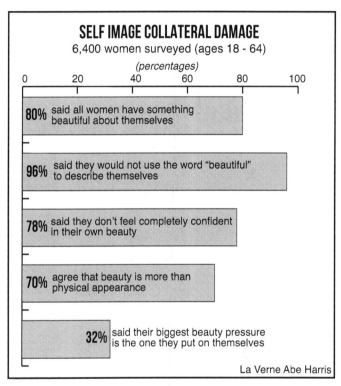

SELF IMAGE COLLATERAL DAMAGE
6,400 women surveyed (ages 18 - 64)
(percentages)

0   20   40   60   80   100

80% said all women have something beautiful about themselves

96% said they would not use the word "beautiful" to describe themselves

78% said they don't feel completely confident in their own beauty

70% agree that beauty is more than physical appearance

32% said their biggest beauty pressure is the one they put on themselves

La Verne Abe Harris

Source: 2015 Dove's Choose Beautiful campaign

A 2ND ACT: INTRODUCTION

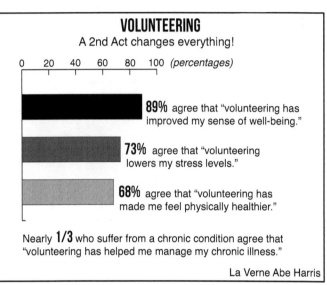

VOLUNTEERING
A 2nd Act changes everything!

0   20   40   60   80   100   *(percentages)*

89% agree that "volunteering has improved my sense of well-being."

73% agree that "volunteering lowers my stress levels."

68% agree that "volunteering has made me feel physically healthier."

Nearly **1/3** who suffer from a chronic condition agree that "volunteering has helped me manage my chronic illness."

La Verne Abe Harris

Source: 2010 United Healthcare/Volunteer Match survey of more than 4,500 Americans about volunteering.

THE MISSION AND WORK OF A2NDACT.ORG

Our Mission: Recognizing that helping is healing, we support and celebrate women survivors of ALL cancers using their gifts of time and experience to give back to the greater good.
Our Work: We are survivors helping survivors take their lives back after cancer.

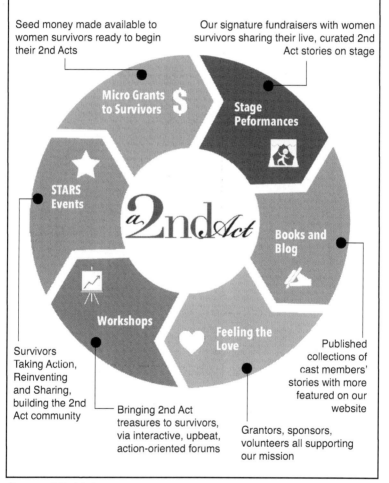

Seed money made available to women survivors ready to begin their 2nd Acts

Our signature fundraisers with women survivors sharing their live, curated 2nd Act stories on stage

Survivors Taking Action, Reinventing and Sharing, building the 2nd Act community

Bringing 2nd Act treasures to survivors, via interactive, upbeat, action-oriented forums

Grantors, sponsors, volunteers all supporting our mission

Published collections of cast members' stories with more featured on our website

Sources: A 2nd Act

Judy is off to the next show...

Judy Pearson, Founder

CHAPTER **1**

JUDY PEARSON
Triple Negative Breast Cancer Survivor

Judy is a writer, speaker, and the founder of A2ndAct. org. She exists happily – loving each day more than the last – at the foot of the Phoenix Mountain Preserve with her husband, David, and their rescued chocolate lab, Izzy Belle.

I wasn't chosen as homecoming queen. This was the most disastrous event to befall my then 17 years on this earth.

My mother, a woman of wisdom who sprinkled chestnuts of inspiration on us frequently, said: "God is saving you for something better."

Of course she was right. Six months later, better arrived: I was selected as the 1971 National Blueberry Queen. I don't know if you've ever met royalty before, but I'll be happy to shake your hand after the performance.

Fast forward to a day in December 2010, when I received a happy gram from my doctor: "Congratulations, your mammogram was clear. See you next year." So imagine my surprise when, lying in bed with my new husband watching television, I discovered a lump in my cleavage.

I asked him to feel it - most men will feel your boobs if you ask them to and he confirmed it was indeed something new.

Two months later, I was diagnosed with the same cancer that killed my mother's sister – triple negative breast cancer. VERY aggressive cancer, the surgeon said, requiring VERY aggressive treatment.

I trooped through a mastectomy – yes they're fake, the real ones tried to kill me! – and 18 rounds of chemo.

And here's the interesting thing – surgeons found four more tumors orbiting the mother ship. Cancer had already begun to spread. Had the big tumor been buried deeper in my breast, I would never have found it in time. My cancer would have probably taken me out as it had my aunt.

So why had I survived? Ironically, my mother's words came back to me: God was saving me for something better. But what?

I'm a non-fiction writer by profession. I do lots of research and had thoroughly researched my disease and my treatment. At NO time did I expect survivorship to be any different than my life before cancer.

Boy was I wrong! Night sweats and joint pain. Insomnia AND chronic fatigue. Brain fog and forgetfulness. And my issues were nothing compared to other survivors I questioned. And the big question for all of us: what purpose did our cancer have in our lives?

But I learned something else from the hundreds of survivors I met: they were doing amazing things.

Regardless of whether they had no evidence of disease, or they were living with their cancer, they were giving back to the greater good. By helping others, they were healing themselves.

And that's not just a cute phrase. There's an ever-growing body of scientific research supporting that theory.

You know, men and women heal very differently. Women are hardwired to be communicative, collaborative, and nurturing. Those traits help us to heal. Men are hardwired to ... men are hardwired to ... Well, their hardwiring isn't relevant here. But it's a fact, if you can get women on board for something, the men will get on board too.

As survivors, we don't need a law or a constitutional amendment to give us our pre-cancer lives back. Most of us like our post cancer lives better anyway! We simply need to hear one another's stories.

And thus, A2ndAct.org was born.

An organization of survivors helping survivors take their lives back after a cancer diagnosis.

Our sole purpose is to help women survivors change their life question from "Why me?" to "What next?"

Our work includes performances like these, allowing us to showcase other non-profits. We work with the medical community and others, offering our ground-breaking 2nd Act workshops. These workshops help survivors discover how their passions, skills and cancer have uniquely qualified them to give back to the greater good. We host Girls Night Out events, survivor networking shindigs just for the fun of it. We publish our own book, a continually growing collection of the stories told on our stage. And in a shameless act of self-promotion, I encourage you to purchase LOTS of them after the show! The book includes the stories you've just heard, and I'll bet this cast and those from previous shows who are here will sign them for you. Bam, holiday shopping done!

Best of all, all other money we raise allows us to make micro grants to local women survivors ready to launch their own 2nd Acts, but who are in need of a little seed money.

Are you getting it? It's an amazing pay it forward love fest!

These 2nd Act stories are our new drugs. These performances are our new treatments and will help us to live our best lives in the time we have left. I mean truthfully, we're all terminal, even if you've never had cancer. Even all of you!

I am humbled by the love and support I've received from my darling husband, my wonderful family and friends, the amazing survivors, our sponsors and all the generous people like you.

To all of you, I will be eternally grateful. Because you see, THIS is my 2nd Act!

CHAPTER **1:** JUDY PEARSON

CHAPTER 2

DIEDRE KAYE
Colon Cancer Survivor

As Diedre was concluding her treatment for stage 4 colon cancer, she found herself in the audience of the inaugural Phoenix production of A 2nd Act: Survivorship Takes the Stage. And she was hooked! A theatre veteran, she now gladly volunteers her time as a member of the board and the performance's Executive Producer.

CHAPTER **2:** DIEDRE KAYE

It was May 22, 2016, the date of the inaugural A 2nd Act Phoenix performance, when I first realized the importance of having a "2nd" act. Tear stains still glistened on my cheeks as I reflected on the stories I had just heard. I was challenged: what would be "next" for me?

I had just finished my last round of chemo for stage IV colon cancer with metastases to my liver and a lymph node above my left lung. I was awaiting my final scan to confirm that the cancer had been stabilized, but I was strongly feeling that all would be good. I had already booked a two-week get-away to San Diego with my husband, Alexx, so we could celebrate the end of the crazy ride we had been on since September 10,, 2015, when our lives were thrown a curve by the cancer diagnosis.

Alexx and I love adventure, even more so when it's together. We didn't marry until our 40's and unlike many newlyweds that age, it was the first marriage for both of us. As neither of us wanted children, it was easy to plan our adventures. Whether it was creating businesses, traveling, or planning the best parties, we always did it with pizzazz.

At the time of my diagnosis, we were in the third summer of what we had hoped to be 10 summers of traveling around the country in our 35-foot Class A motorhome. To that date, we had managed to "camp" in 38 states, see all 30 major league baseball parks, and attend just as many theatrical performances all over

CHAPTER **2**: DIEDRE KAYE

the country, including nine Broadway shows. We had already started planning our next outing which would take us to Halifax, Nova Scotia, on the Atlantic Ocean, turn left, and then blast our way through Canada to Vancouver and the Pacific Ocean. But that trip was not to be.

My doctors had determined that it was in my best interest to do 12 rounds of chemo and thereafter continue every three weeks with an immunotherapy drug. My infusions would always be done in Phoenix so my doctors could continue to monitor my cancer. They said I couldn't expect to be cured, but we could manage my cancer so that I would have a good quality of life. That sounded fair to us, but it meant we no longer could take off for endless RV trips. We said good-bye to "Air Barty One," our motorhome, but we did not say good-bye to travel. We would just need to plan it between infusions. It seemed to be a small concession for having a good quality of life.

I decided to chronicle the ups and downs of my cancer journey with a blog on the Caring Bridge website. My commitment to myself and my followers was to write every day for 200 days. I never missed a day, no matter how I felt, even if it was just to say, "I'll write more tomorrow."

When I returned home from our San Diego trip, I received the report from the doctor that I expected. There was no evidence of disease in my colon, liver, or lymph node. YES! We were all ready to rejoice. Cards and calls flooded in with everyone's excitement. My 200 day blog would now end and life could return to normal ... or so I thought.

CHAPTER **2:** DIEDRE KAYE

For some unknown reason, life seemed incomplete now, and I wasn't sure why. I had already retired from successful careers in education, business and theater. What more could I possibly want? But a force kept pulling at me asking the question, "How are you going to give back for all that has been given to you this past year?"

Not only had friends and family showered me with love far beyond what I had ever imagined, but the reality was, I was still alive. For some reason, I had been spared. Echoing in the back of my mind were all those stories I had heard at the A 2nd Act performance by women who had found their way to give back. I wanted to feel what they felt ... to know what they knew about helping others. There must be something I could do to fill this void. I needed my "2nd Act." Friends encouraged me to continue my writing. Many said I had inspired them with my blog and hoped I would make it a book. I signed up for a writing class at the Virginia Piper Cancer Center. I thought it would be worth attending if it could just get me inspired to start writing again.

In the "it's a small world" category, the workshop presenter was the founder of A2ndAct.org, Judy Pearson. Little did I know, that it was Judy who embodied the force that was pulling me. By the end of the workshop, I was as impressed with this woman as I was the production last May. Through her research, she had found that women survivors helping others helped to heal themselves as well. And that's exactly what I wanted to do – help others like me, and continue to heal myself in the process.

I had planned to contact Judy and see how I might be of service to her organization. After all, I had backgrounds in education, marketing, administration, and theater. There must be something I could do to make a difference, I thought.

I left the workshop with my head spinning. I didn't know what was happening, but somehow I knew there was something more important about this workshop than me writing a book.

As I walked to my car, I noticed Judy walking out the side door of the building and going in my same direction. Oh! I thought. I can tell her right now! So I did. I expressed how appreciative I was of the performance that she had organized. I asked her about "A2A" (as I call it) and about her staff. With a wry smile, she replied, "Staff, hmmm. You're pretty much looking at it."

Although she had some volunteers and funding to help out, she worked alone. As I wanted to do something to contribute, I asked if she needed help. I was in the process of selling our home and was still in recovery myself, plus I was in training for a half-marathon, but, oh well, I would find some time to help if I could. I don't think I had finished my sentence before she threw her arms around me and asked when we could meet to discuss what I would like to do. Oh, yes. She was a force.

Within a short time we were chatting and planning on

CHAPTER **2:** DIEDRE KAYE

a weekly basis. New marketing focus, independence, grants, and expansion were all topics we covered.

Fast forward to the present: we have just celebrated the third Phoenix performance and soon our third Tucson performance. As I write this, we are planning the path for A 2nd Act performances to be held in locations beyond Arizona, including Canada! I have the honor of being the "rudder" for the organization – keeping us on track as Judy continues to generate many great ideas.

It must be infectious as I now offer a good share of my own ideas. And ever since we established ourselves as a 501(c)(3) organization, I have proudly served as one of the members of the Board of Directors. I am the Executive Producer for the performances which means I help with all aspects of the productions including my favorite job, coaching the participants to be the best presenters they can be.

At the end of each performance, I feel the same depth of emotion that I felt at the 2016 Phoenix performance. But now I am filled with the satisfaction of knowing I have found my 2nd act. New cancer cells have gathered in my lungs, but they are small and very slow to grow. I expect to have many more years of celebration, but no matter what, I am healing and helping others to heal, because of my 2nd act – which is A 2nd Act!

TUCSON

In the shadows of the Santa Catalina mountains, these women trudged through the darkest hours of cancer. But the disease did not defeat them. Rather it touched their lives in ways they never might have imagined, giving them a new appreciation for every sunrise, and making them stronger and more dedicated in their 2nd Acts.

Sunday, November 13, 2016, 2:00 p.m
Berger Center for the Performing Arts, Tucson, AZ
❦

This performance was made possible by the generosity of Radiation Ltd., Printex, KVOA and MIXfm.

Love to Mrs. Grant, Emcee
MIXfm Morning Mix

Tucson cast members from left to right:
LaNita Price, Karen Conway, Isabelle Barbour, Susan Kinkade, Judy Pearson,
Sara Moore, Lisa Reynolds, Ginny Williams

CHAPTER 3

GINNY WILLIAMS
Breast Cancer Survivor

Ginny lived in a coal-mining town in northeastern Pennsylvania until college. There, she earned a B.S., an M.Ed. and an Ed.D degree all in support of her teaching career. She retired from education in 2006 and moved to Arizona, where she works with Southern Arizona Greyhound Adoption. Learn more at *www. sagreyhoundadoption.org.*

CHAPTER 3: GINNY WILLIAMS

The day of my needle biopsy was the day that I decided that I was going to beat cancer rather than the other way around. There was just no way that cancer was going to take over my life. So, I did what I had planned for that day.

I went to the vet's to pick up (and I mean that literally) a newly spayed greyhound, lifted her into the back of an SUV and took her to her foster home.

And then, two days after my lumpectomy a few weeks later, I did a six mile walk. Normally, I would have taken a hike instead, but I thought that might have been too much, too soon. As it was, my walk was a big mistake.

I bruised so badly that it actually scared me. So, I called my surgeon immediately, and she told me to come right in. The first thing she said to me was: "What have you done?" When I told her, she said that the word "walk" in the post-op instructions meant just around the block – not six miles. OOPS!

So, I went back to doing what I've been doing for almost 20 years – taking care of greyhounds that have just gotten off the track. I'd clean their kennels, feed them and best of all, play with them.

As soon as the dogs would come into our intake kennel, we'd de-tick and de-flea them and give them baths. You just can't imagine how they would respond! Sometimes it was almost as though they went into sleep mode they were so relaxed. At other times they'd respond with a sudden burst of energy and pure joy.

I was just so delighted to be part of their transformation and the beginning of their new lives. For me, it was the best cancer support ever! And I realized then that the rescued greyhounds were a lot like cancer survivors. They, too, had to endure some harsh treatment just as cancer patients suffer through chemo and radiation.

But, at the end of it all, we both have a new appreciation for life. It's a joie de vivre that we have in common and an honor for me to help them begin their 2nd Acts of life.

As you've most likely surmised by now, I also had a pet greyhound at home. His name was Lincoln, and he was truly "my dog." Initially, like many of us survivors, I had a difficult time accepting my diagnosis, so I was often awake at night. But, if I was up so too was Lincoln.

He'd sit beside me and look at me with his doe-like eyes. if I went to take a shower, he'd be lying just outside the bathroom door – all 87 pounds of him! While I lost Lincoln soon after I began chemo, I will never forget him or the love and concern that he had for me.

Because hiking has always been therapy for me, I hit the trails again while in chemo. I began slowly with shorter hikes as I didn't have the same energy level that I once did. It was on one of those hikes when a

CHAPTER 3: GINNY WILLIAMS

gal in my hiking group turned to me and said, "You know, you look a lot better than I thought you would." I took that as a compliment because I was even paler then than I am right now!

When I finished treatment and got back some of my energy, I was off on hiking trips that took me to Alaska, Utah and New Mexico. A few weeks ago, I was in Colorado, hiking in snow at 12,500 feet. And, I can't wait to go again!

Until then, though, I'll continue helping newly arrived greyhounds transition to life as someone's pet.
And, even though it's not a mission that is new to me, it means more to me now than ever before. It affords me the opportunity to give back to a breed that has given me so much during this time in my life.

As I look back now, I laugh about some of the things that have happened – my misunderstanding of my surgeon's use of the word "walk" and the left-handed compliment of a fellow hiker. And then there was the trip to the dentist in Nogales, Mexico.

As I was coming through customs, I handed an officious-looking border patrol officer my open passport. He looked at my picture, at me, and then back at my picture once again. Obviously, that pre-cancer picture didn't look much like the person standing before him. I finally said, "That picture was taken before chemo when I had a lot more hair." He softened, smiled and said, "You're a survivor. Good for you."

CHAPTER **3:** GINNY WILLIAMS

I think that if that same border patrol officer were here today he'd say, "You're all survivors. Good for you!"

CHAPTER **3:** GINNY WILLIAMS

CHAPTER 4

SUSAN KINKADE
Leukemia Cancer Survivor

Susan is a wife, mother, emergency nurse and cancer warrior. She volunteers for the "Be The Match" bone marrow program, as well as with the American Cancer Society Relay for Life. She speaks to nursing and medical students about her experience on the other side of the hospital bed. Learn more about bone marrow donation at *www.bethematch.org*.

CHAPTER **4:** SUSAN KINKADE

Close your eyes for a minute. Imagine yourself as an emergency nurse who has helped people in their darkest hour for over 30 years. Imagine you haven't been to your doctor for ages because, well, you're a nurse and you know what's going on with your health.

Imagine you went in for some blood work prior to an elective surgery but only because it was required. Imagine waking up after a well-deserved nap on a Friday afternoon and hearing a message on your voice mail from your doctor saying, "If you are still my patient you need to make an appointment right away because you have some abnormal lab work that we need to talk about!"

My Monday morning appointment couldn't come soon enough. In one short conversation I heard three words that changed my life — you have leukemia. Chemotherapy and radiation would treat it, but a bone marrow transplant was my only hope for a complete cure.

Early on, I wanted to keep my diagnosis private. I felt that if I admitted I was sick, I'd have people feeling sorry for me. I didn't want to go to a support group where I was afraid I'd see hopeless people. I struggled with my choice, but everything changed the day I made the decision to go public.

They say it takes a village to walk with you down the cancer road. I found it takes many villages.

CHAPTER **4**: SUSAN KINKADE

I had my family village, my work village, my community village and my church village. Everyone intertwined to support me and my family and carry me in my weak moments.

I met people I never would have met otherwise. I've become closer than ever before to others.

My detour through the valley of leukemia was certainly not all rainbows and roses. Was I scared? Absolutely! I needed stem cells from bone marrow to survive! Being a bone marrow donor is a huge commitment.

The only thing that scared me more than the diagnosis was the thought that my three brothers who live out of state wouldn't agree to bone marrow donor testing. Or if they did, none would be a match. Fortunately, they all agreed and one WAS a perfect match. It's times like this when you really find out how important family is.

Did I go through dark times? Most definitely! I embraced and acknowledged the bad times and chose to move on and celebrate the good things that came my way. A few symbolic items have helped carry me through my journey and will always remain close to me.

When I went in the hospital for my transplant, I asked my husband to find a special rock that I could hold to remind me of him. He has been my true rock and fortress from day one. That rock sits on my desk at work to remind me of how far I've come and the strength and love that he has given me.

As I was walking out the doors of the hospital on discharge day, on my way to a new life, the social worker slipped a small key into my hand. She said, "You earned this." The key has the word "strength" written on it. It took me a while to understand the symbolism of that simple word. Now I do: that key symbolizes the key to life after leukemia. It was up to me to open the door to that new life and begin my 2nd Act.

One of the most important lessons I learned on my journey was patience — with myself, my family and my health care team.

In the early days after my transplant, I was physically weak but mentally strong. I would set small goals for myself like walking to the end of the block or going to church.

As my leash at the cancer center became a little longer, I gained strength and started doing hikes and planning little trips. I continued trying to define what my new normal and my 2nd Act would be.

Six months after my transplant, I got to travel to Oklahoma for my son's graduation from basic training. I felt like I was on the vacation of a lifetime. I was doing what normal people do!

One year after my diagnosis, I was given clearance to return to work, as long as I didn't have direct patient contact.

The bedside nurse in me really struggled with that but I was able to define "nurse" in a different way. As a trauma outreach coordinator, I transitioned from being an ER nurse to being in the community teaching injury prevention.

On my one year transplant anniversary, I felt like I had conquered the world. I wanted affirmation that I was alive and well. How did I celebrate? I went sky diving! Reaching out and touching the sky was an amazing moment, although probably not the smartest thing to do for someone who has no platelets!

From way up there in the sky, I could feel myself heading back to life's main road and knew that I wanted to spread the message that there is life after cancer. That would be my 2nd Act.

Being on the other side of the hospital bed gave me a whole new perspective of what a patient goes through. Using my experience, I speak to nursing and medical students giving them a view they wouldn't typically get in school.

I also speak to bone marrow transplant patients. They hear about the whole transplant process from their health care team, but sharing my journey gives them encouragement. I give them a "Walk to Wellness" packet that has a pedometer and journal in it.

Hearing that attitude and exercise play a huge part in

their recovery is good medicine, and helps them see that while the road is long, there is light at the end of the tunnel.

People have asked me, "At what point do you start counting how long you've survived? My survival started the day I received my diagnosis. It was when I made the affirmation to fight and go where this detour in my life's journey would lead me.

Early on, my doctor and I made a pact that I wouldn't look at research that showed life expectancy after my type of cancer. I have kept that promise. To this day, I don't know how long I'm expected to live.

But to be fair, who among us really does? I feel like each of us is unique and will travel our own journey, regardless of the statistics. I'm not just surviving – I'm thriving! I have made the choice to live every day like it matters.

I have to say that while skydiving was on my bucket list, leukemia certainly wasn't! But as a result of my disease, I have a new passion for life and can't wait to see what the future holds.

Embrace your journey and take each day a step at a time. Let yourself be open to the help of those around you. Celebrate the little things. Live YOUR life like it matters!

CHAPTER **4**: SUSAN KINKADE

CHAPTER 5

LISA REYNOLDS
Childhood Thyroid Cancer Survivor

Lisa, a resident of Tucson, has been a patient navigator for the American Cancer Society for the past six years. She is an advocate for the American Cancer Society's Cancer Action Network and advocates for more funding for cancer research. She also participates in Relay For Life. Learn more at *www.cancer.org.*

CHAPTER 5: LISA REYNOLDS

It was 1981. I was 8 and my family was on the way down to Mexico to go sailing. My brother and I were in the back seat doing what siblings do: having an argument.

He said, "You're ugly." So I, of course, responded the same. Then he said, "Well, you have a lump in your neck." And I of course said, "Well, you have a lump in your neck." My mom turned around quickly and said, "Where?" My brother pointed and said, "Right there." And I pointed at him and said, "Yeah, right there."

That was the day I found out boys have Adam's apples and girls don't. In fact, girls aren't supposed to have lumps in their necks at all.

My mom called my doctor when we got home from our trip. His advice was not to worry about the lump' to "just wait and see what happens."

Luckily, my mother didn't listen. She took me to her ear, nose, and throat doctor. The next thing I knew, I was seeing a pediatric surgeon, and a lumpectomy was scheduled.

Following my lumpectomy, I was only able to eat broth and jello. Doctors had finally promised me a milkshake, but before it arrived, we got the news. Thyroid cancer. My mother fainted. I didn't know what cancer was, and I wondered if it meant I wasn't getting my milkshake. And I didn't get one.

CHAPTER **5:** LISA REYNOLDS

Instead, I got scheduled for a total thyroidectomy to be performed a few days later. The cancer was in both sides of my thyroid and had spread to my windpipe. So ... it would be surgery and the protocol of the day: a large dose of radioactive iodine.

I had always felt a little bit like an outcast as a child. Getting thyroid cancer at a young age certainly solidified that. It was not a normal childhood cancer. I didn't have normal childhood treatment, and I wasn't in the childhood oncology unit for treatment.

I was in nuclear medicine, the bomb shelter of the hospital. My treatment came in a lead container that no one was supposed to go near. There was a tiny bottle inside that they squirted water in and I drank. Seemed safe.

Once I was able, I went back to school. But having just gone through surgery for cancer, no one would sit by me. Some of the kids were afraid they might catch cancer, too.

Others asked if I smoked. About this time, there was a big anti-smoking campaign going on. As kids, we didn't understand the difference between lung cancer and any other kind, so they all just assumed I was puffing away during recess.

Over the next two years, my cancer was controlled. But then we got word that it had spread to my lungs and my lymph nodes.

CHAPTER 5: LISA REYNOLDS

In scans, the spots on my lungs looked like lights on a Christmas tree. Decisions had to be made. After some research on my doctor's part. Despite my age, I was now 10, he recommended I receive the maximum adult dose of radioactive iodine.

Because I gave off radioactivity, I was in a hospital isolation unit, with a sign on my door that said, "Caution. Radiation." I was the radiation!

They taped a safety line around my bed, indicating how far back people had to stay to not be exposed. Every few hours, a team would come in with a Geiger counter to test me, and as my radioactivity diminished, they'd move the tape back.

My dad was excited about all of this. Because of emitting so much radioactivity, he figured he wouldn't have to put up Christmas lights up that year. They could just put me on the roof and Santa would find his way.

I was in fifth grade when I was finally declared in remission. And I guess that's the moment my 2nd Act began. I wanted to volunteer as much as I was able given my age. I mostly raised money for the American Cancer Society and the Arizona Cancer Center. But I often felt like a fish out of water.

By the time I turned 16, I had never met another child who had cancer. When I would tell people that I had had cancer, they would ask, "Oh, leukemia?" I would tell them no and they would either lose interest or ask, "Did you lose your hair?" Again I would say no and usually received a look suggesting maybe I didn't really have cancer.

When I first started seeing childhood cancer events, I didn't go. I didn't fit in. Even when I offered to volunteer with other kids who had cancer, they put me with the siblings of cancer patients. Only the kids with normal childhood cancer could relate to current patients. It was assumed I couldn't.

So I volunteered at Arizona Camp Sunrise Sidekicks, a camp for brothers and sisters of kids with cancer. The upside of this was that I learned what it must have been like for my brother when I had gone through treatment.

I was able to do that for five years, until migraines caused me to stop. There's a lot of physical fallout when you don't have a thyroid: rapid heart rate, depression, and migraines as well.

Having gone through two diagnoses, surgeries and hospitalizations, and of course, my "glow" juice treatment (radioactive iodine), I had decided at a young age that I was going to be the one to cure cancer. But my brain wasn't on board.

So, I decided to advocate for money to fund those whose brains were on board! That is when I joined the American Cancer Society Cancer Action Network.

CHAPTER 5: LISA REYNOLDS

I have been to both the State Capitol and Washington D.C. to lobby for increased funding for cancer research.

I continued volunteering at different places and then was lucky enough to be hired by the Ronald McDonald House as a weekend manager.

Then six years ago, my 2nd Act dream came true. A job with the American Cancer Society! Now, I work as a patient navigator, helping patients find the resources they need to get their treatment.

I am so glad to do what I do, but I never feel like I've done enough. There aren't support groups for adults of unusual childhood cancers and we often don't feel as though we fit in to the adult cancer survivor world.

Even the medical world doesn't know how to deal with me. A doctor once called to tell me my tumor marker was high. He didn't know what that meant. I did. It meant I had cancer again.

More blood tests and and a chest x-ray, where the technician asked why I was having a chest x-ray. I told her I had had metastatic thyroid cancer as a child and they thought it had come back. Her response: "Are they sure it was cancer?"

I remembered my two surgeries and multiple radioactive iodine treatments, and replied, "They seemed pretty sure."

I want to help change that. I want to see a day where there are no more children being diagnosed with cancer. And if they are, I want to see them have fewer long-term effects, something I'm so very familiar with.

Many childhood cancer survivors can not have children. In fact, I was told I could not have children. Luckily, this was another time in my life that a doctor was wrong. My 10-year-old son is right here in the audience as proof!

So, the fight goes on and my work goes on. I hope this view from another perspective, a voice from another kind of cancer survivor, will also help you understand my passion … my drive … my 2nd Act!

CHAPTER **6**

LANITA PRICE
Breast Cancer Survivor

LaNita, a native of Florida, retired from the Air Force in May 2007 and moved to Tucson with her husband Vaughn. They have one daughter and two grandchildren. She is a graduate of Park University with a BS in Social Psychology and a Masters in Addiction Counseling from Grand Canyon University. LaNita has worked in the counseling field and is a licensed minister. She uses her licensure and degrees to help provide life coaching through Healing Hearts Ministries.

What do you do when your slip is hanging?

Funny question I know. But I grew up in Florida and my elders used that saying when someone appeared to have it all together. And then something happened they did not want the world to see.

That was me!

I had been single and celibate for 11 and a half years until I met my now husband. I dressed nice, smelled nice. I had conquered the Air Force and retired as a single mom. I had a nice vehicle, good friends and people labeled me as a good friend and person. I had all the external things that gave me the image I thought I wanted to convey.

Then, in November 2012, the storm came. The wind blew and the ME I had known and loved would change forever and not by choice. Suddenly and without warning, MY slip was about to hang.

I found myself between a rock and hard place when the doctor called me in for my mammogram results. Oddly enough she asked me, "What do you think your results are?"

I said, "Well it can't be good, since they would not give them to me over the phone." She stated that her normal protocol is to have the patient come in and talk with her no matter what the results were.

She then looked me in the eyes and said, "I'm sorry but you have breast cancer Stage II and the surgeons want to operate as soon as possible."

I remember how the tears streamed down my face. On the inside I kept asking, "Me? Are they sure? Me?" The doctor hugged me tightly and told me it would be alright and someone would be contacting me soon to schedule surgery.

As I walked out in the hot Arizona sun, my thoughts and heart went immediately to my husband, Vaughn. We'd only been married five years at this point. He was a widower, whose first wife of 13 years, Yolanda, had died in 2004 due to complications from ovarian cancer treatment.

I never once thought of death, but two big balloons of concern floated into my mind.

First, not only did my husband have to go through his first wife's cancer treatment and death, but now his second wife had cancer too.

And secondly, how was my body going to change? Would I lose my hair? One or both of my breasts? Would nausea, weight loss, loss of energy and who knows what else plague me?

And what would other people think? You know when the big "C" word is said to someone, whether to the patient or anyone else hearing it, more often than not people immediately assign a death sentence.

CHAPTER **6:** LANITA PRICE

I called my mom and sister before I talked with my husband. Their reactions were far from what I expected. They immediately began to speak faith, not fear, the complete opposite of what their first response would have been in times past. It blessed me how much their faith had grown and I knew I could count on their support.

As I shared with them my questions and concerns, what I heard was "All is well; faith not fear." To this day I have not thought any differently.

It was finally time to call my husband. He voiced what I had already heard from my sister and mom. "All is well; we will get through this." My heart ached for him and the fact that he would once again be thrown into the role of provider and caregiver, but something on the inside knew that if I had to go through this, then he is the one I wanted by my side!

Our daughter, Brittney, had told us just a few weeks earlier that she was pregnant with our first grandchild. So it took several days before I shared my diagnosis with her.

Since then, we now have two beautiful grandchildren: our little prince Noel who is three, and our princess Aria who just turned one.

While there are so many things that have taken place throughout all of this, I can truly say that God and His word, coupled with friends and family, and even complete strangers placed in my path, have been a

CHAPTER **6**: LANITA PRICE

43

source of strength and encouragement.

My journey after diagnosis began with a lumpectomy in December of 2012. Two weeks later, I was told that there were more cancer cells and I would need an additional surgery, so 28 days after the first surgery I was under the knife again having a mastectomy.

I finished chemotherapy that summer and then began several months of radiation.

It has taken a series of five surgeries to put "Patchwork Patti" – my affectionate name for myself – back together again.

My testimony is that, through all of this, I can still smile. My faith never wavered. I am so very thankful for the friends, family, coworkers and strangers I have met along the way.

So now it's my turn to pay it forward. Cancer treatment stripped away a lot of layers of the "me" I thought I needed to be.

Now with the new me, I work harder at trying to pay attention to life and those around me. My 2nd Act after my journey has allowed me to become a life coach for women who have areas in their lives where they are stuck, distracted, unfocused, unsure, and even unmotivated to change.

Through Healing Hearts Ministry, I offer my services

to those in my local church and those referred to me who do not attend. I've found that sickness and disease are not the only distractors that cause us to get off track and lose our identity and life purpose. We as women spend so much time caring for others, that we fail ourselves.

I have a friend who found herself in that rut for a while when she ran across a book called The Intentional Woman by an Arizona author. She introduced me to the book. Together we were so impressed by how it was impacting our own lives, we created a group that will come together for six weeks, helping women unpack their issues, find the power of their story and help them to live it out loud.

While I find it very rewarding to help others, I in no way profess to have it all together. What I do profess is that I refuse to stay down and I ALWAYS fight to get back up and find a 2nd Act.

So what did I do with that slip of mine that was hanging?

I took it off! I wave it now as my flag, my reminder that what I thought mattered doesn't. And what I was concerned that people would see is exactly what they NEED to see. I am a walking testament that no matter what comes your way, you can weather the storm!

CHAPTER 7

SARA THERESE MOORE
AML Cancer Survivor

Sara is a photographer, artist, writer, and now - cancer survivor. With the soul of a gypsy, she's backpacked through 29 countries on five continents; most recently traveling solo in a 17 foot travel trailer. She has chosen to share her leukemia journey as part of her travel blog, Sarandipity Travels, hoping her transparency in writing will help others cope with their own struggles. Learn more at *www.sarandipitytravels.com*.

I'm very new to being a cancer survivor, but not new to surviving. You see, I watched my mother battle leukemia from the time I was 10 years old until I laid in bed with her as a teenager and watched her take her last breath.

In 2004, I found my son, shortly after his 15th birthday, dead on the couch due to suicide. This was followed by my sister's passing in 2010, and most recently, my husband's death in January of this year while I was in the midst of fighting my newly diagnosed cancer.

I can tell you this with a peaceful heart, because each loved one has had a profound impact on me. In their life and in their death, they have helped to shape who I am.

And I like who I am. Long ago I stopped asking "Why me?" I live by the motto, "It is what it is, but it will become what you make of it."

While talking with my daughter one day last fall, shortly after my diagnosis, she encouraged me to share my cancer journey with the world through my blog: Sarandipity Travels.

I took her advice and my hope has been that being transparent in my writing will help others cope with their own struggles. It is a part of my 2nd Act.

We all have a story to tell and being vulnerable enough to bare our souls so we can be fully embraced and understood, is one of the most beautiful experiences in life. Please allow me to share some of my blog entries with you.

Oct. 9th, 2015
Day 5 and still no diagnosis ....
I lay in the dark in my hospital room, silent tears rolling down my face. They follow the path of previous tears and I don't bother to wipe them away.

Yesterday was my hardest day. It started with a wave of dizziness, followed by pain in my chest, as I struggled to get my breath. A rush of doctors and nurses surrounded me, while my father and stepmom stood quietly to one side. A respiratory therapist tried to give me a mask but my hand shook and I couldn't find my face.

Later, I could hear my step-mom asking questions of the hospitalist quietly outside the cracked door.

"I'm sorry. She's very, very sick," was the only response I heard.

Now, in the quiet of the night, I cried... not for myself, but for my daughter and parents. I knew what it meant to lose a mother, and I knew what it meant to lose a child. It wasn't supposed to be like this.

The blue of the night was replaced by the warm light of dawn peeking through the crooked slats of my window. The flow of doctors and nurses would soon begin, each entering my room with masks and kind eyes that hinted at their hidden smiles.

Sprinkled between these visits were medications, blood draws, bone marrow biopsies, and the sound of my family's cheerful voices. They told stories to fill the silent hours and lighten the heaviness that crowded the corners of my thoughts.

The soft spoken oncologist entered my room and I could see it pained him to tell me he didn't have news on my biopsy yet. For the next half an hour, he answered all of the questions I asked; questions based in fear followed by answers I didn't hear.

Day 11 and two young doctors confirm my suspicion of leukemia. They smiled when they told me I had acute promyelocytic leukemia, and at first I thought their upbeat demeanor was a way of softening the bad news. But they seemed truly excited.

"You don't understand. This is a good thing! This is the most curable form of AML leukemia there is! It's very aggressive, but also very rare and very treatable." In that moment, I began to sob. These were tears of joy, and I said the most heartfelt prayer I've ever said. "Thank you, God!"

Dec. 25th, 2015
I spent Christmas morning getting chemo. My treatment plan calls for 110 chemo infusions and there were no breaks for holidays. I was given the beautiful gift of poison, wrapped in a clear plastic bag, hanging on a pole just for me; a gift bag of arsenic that

I'm so thankful to receive. It made me think about the irony of it all.

Society loves a triumphant, positive hero. It makes us feel good to see someone fight and win, and stay strong through it all.

It's much harder to see someone rage, and fall apart, and admit they're struggling. This scenario puts pressure on the cancer patient to bury their emotions for the benefit of others.

To state the obvious, "this isn't easy!" I'm human, and weak, and often get down in the muck and wallow at how horrible it is.

I get why people resent the word 'gift' and 'cancer' used in the same sentence. Yet after each mud bath of frustration and anger, I slog my way toward the positives. I reach my muddy hand out to receive the gifts because they help me to heal my torn bits.

So what are my gifts of cancer? I've been shown the beauty of the human spirit. Unselfish, compassionate human beings have appeared in abundance. If I ever questioned my worth in this world, I will never do so again. I know I'm loved.

I let the trivial fall away, cherish authentic relationships, live and speak my truth. I'm quick to hug, and slow to leave. I value kindness above all else.

CHAPTER **7: SARA THERESE MOORE**

We don't know when our time on this earth will end. Cancer took the distant death deadline that I never thought about, and shoved it in my face for examination.

Remission has allowed me to distance myself from the inevitable once again, but keeps my mortality present enough to appreciate each day.

In a very real and powerful way, I know that today is a gift and in my 2nd Act, I recognize the perfection in all experiences.

Now, I travel the nation, a solo female in her tiny travel trailer, camera in one hand, pen and paper in another, experiencing life to it's fullest and sharing a piece of my soul with others, in the hopes that they, too, can create a 2nd Act after their life struggles.

The good news is that none of these lessons need come from experiencing cancer. In fact, much of this I already knew. But, leukemia has been the catalyst in reminding me: To Love. To feel. To travel. To take risks. To be gentle with myself. And ultimately, to connect on a deeper level.

Thank you, Cancer. Now, get lost!

CHAPTER 8

ISABELLE SUE BARBOUR
Breast and Ovarian Cancer Survivor

Isabelle's first book, *A Woman Under Construction,* offers readers a road map of her journey through diagnosis and treatment for breast cancer. Now in treatment for ovarian cancer, Isabelle thanks her family and especially her husband, Duane-Rafe, for all the years of help and support.

The most shattering phone call I've ever received came in 2005. "I'm so sorry, Isabelle," said my doctor. "It's breast cancer. You will have to go to surgery." Thus started an odyssey that continues to this day.

The next step took my husband and me to a cancer center where, as far as I could tell, everyone was speaking in tongues. They seemed to think we should be in a hurry to understand what they were telling us.

There were unfamiliar medical terms, strange sounding tests, options for surgical procedures, clinical trials. On and on the new information went, mostly over our heads. The only thing we heard for sure was that I had a very aggressive type of cancer and didn't have the luxury of dithering around. It had to go.

Decisions had to be made on the spot. A lot of labs, x-rays and tests had to be done, all of which would culminate in some type of devastating surgery. And all in the next few days. I've spent more time dallying over the selection of a new car than on the choices I needed to make to ensure that I would have a future.

Frantic, I visited the cancer center's library in hopes of some guidance from other patients. Prowling the shelves, I looked for information that would help me decide which procedure would be best for me. But sadly, I found no patient stories of any kind.

"Okay," I thought to myself. "If I can't find a road map that works, why don't I create one for other patients coming after me?" And that's exactly what I did, never realizing that I was starting my 2nd Act in the process.

As I proceeded through experimental surgery and chemotherapy, I wrote about what I found along the way. I journaled about what having cancer can do TO you, and as time went by I realized some things about what having cancer can do FOR you.

For instance, I soon learned that cancer doesn't happen just to the patient. It happens to the whole family, to friends, co-workers, neighbors. Everyone feels the impact of a loved one getting cancer.

I wrote it all down, with no clue that I was giving birth to a book. I called it A Woman Under Construction. My original intention was to simply write something to be available to patients in that cancer center's particular library. But thanks to well-meaning friends, my little story found a publisher and wandered off on its own.

Soon I began receiving cards and emails from around the country. I read precious letters thanking me: for helping someone understand a loved one's illness; for helping someone find courage and hope; for unraveling the confusion of a new diagnosis.

Passed hand to hand, my book went where it was needed, with very little help from me. Too ill to participate in any sort of marketing, each letter lifted my own tortured heart and gave me a sense of wonder that my story had helped people navigate the minefields of a cancer diagnosis.

Perhaps the most poignant moment of my whole life occurred one day at a street fair, when a young lady bounced up and threw her arms around me. "I had to meet you," she said. "I saw your picture in that book, A Woman Under Construction." Startled, I agreed that I was indeed the lady in the picture.

"I knew it!" she said. "I want you to know that book saved my life. I couldn't face the thought of having cancer and had decided to go ahead and die. But the social worker brought me your book and asked me to read it before I decided.

"I did, and thought, 'Hey, if she can do it, so can I.' So I had the surgery and all the treatment." She went on, "I just wanted you to meet my husband and our baby, and to thank you for sharing your courage with others."

Turning, she walked away with her husband's arm around her, cure behind her, and her life back. Dumbfounded, I decided I had just heard the best book review there could ever be.

Around that time, I had found that I carry the BRCA gene, and suddenly I was fighting to survive metastatic ovarian cancer. My prognosis was very poor. Simultaneously, my beloved daughter was diagnosed with breast cancer.

Together we went to chemo loaded with craft projects

to see us through those difficult times. We said, "If we are still alive by Christmas, at least we'll have the presents ready!" PAUSE I'm happy to say that my daughter lives, and just celebrated her five-year milestone.

As for me, having ovarian cancer is like having a deadbeat relative. It keeps coming back, PAUSE with its grubby hand out, ready to take more than I have to give. I'm currently on my fifth recurrence. Maybe I'm really just a stubborn old broad, PAUSE but I like to think of myself as a survivor!

It's a hard row to hoe, that's true. Sometimes I lose track of which surgeries I had when, or how many kinds of chemotherapies I've taken. I often forget whether my hair is coming or going PAUSE as I progress through treatment after treatment.

Sometimes I get so tired I would cheerfully lie down on the floor in Walmart if my pride would let me.

Even my own brother said to me, "Boy you sure are taking a long time to die!" PAUSE You gotta love brothers – and I love mine!

But I live, and I love my life every time I see another Christmas or another birthday. A gorgeous morning, or a new baby in the family. Each event is a win; each day is another miracle.

And when I'm worn out in strength or spirit, I think

of those cards and letters from places like Tampa and Bowling Green and Milwaukee, and especially that sweet young lady in Little Rock.

My gift to other cancer patients came right back home to uplift and encourage me to write another book. God willing, my 2nd act will bring comfort and hope to even more people.

CHAPTER 9

KAREN CONWAY
Ovarian Cancer Survivor

Karen was diagnosed three times with ovarian cancer – 11, 10 and nine years ago. She is a member of the Tucson chapter of the National Ovarian Cancer Coalition, helping to bring awareness to this silent killer: "It whispers, so listen." She also attends two other support groups helping others on their cancer journeys.

CHAPTER **9:** **KAREN CONWAY**

Lying in bed in a corner suite, like some kind of a princess. Ha – I didn't even have medical insurance! I kept repeating it over and over. I have cancer ... l have ovarian cancer. OH MY GOD! I'm gonna die! God please don't let me die; I'll do anything you ask!

Like a whirlwind, a haboob, really, there was surgery, chemo, lab tests, CAT scans, MRI's, and new doctors' appointments. Plus, I didn't have a working cell. I couldn't call any of my family since most lived out of town, but they eventually found me.

During treatment, I found a cancer support group.

Two groups, actually, one for gynecological cancers specifically and the other for all women's cancers. What a relief to find other women with similar diagnoses and stories like mine. I don't know what I would have done without them. I've made lifelong friendships from them! They were a blessing beyond compare

My employment situation, on the other hand, was far less than a blessing. Despite my pleas, I lost my temp job because I could not return to work full time immediately after major surgery. Wait, what? That can't be right. I have cancer. I just had major cancer surgery! Can they do that? Apparently they can and did.

Despite my cancer fallout, I refound my passion – and

what would become my 2nd Act – music! I had been involved in choral groups in North Caroline before I moved to Tucson.

First, I joined a women's choral group. Despite chemo and being immune-suppressed, I made rehearsals and even performed in concert with them, bald head and all! (Although I think I wore a scarf.)

Within a year I found a wonderful church choir, led by a doctor of music. Good, I thought, he'll demand it from us, which is what I had previously been used to. But best of all, they were planning a trip to New York City in May of 2007.

Remember the old joke, "How do you get to Carnegie Hall? PRACTICE! PRACTICE! PRACTICE!"

To sing at Carnegie Hall would be a dream come true, a bigger dream than I ever expected in my 2nd Act. Chemo was temporarily stopped and despite being somewhat debilitated from my treatment, I made the trip.

It was so exciting to sing Vivaldi's "Gloria" in that gorgeous hall, where so many famed vocalists and instrumentalists had performed before us. I sat there taking it all in ... ahh ... the ambience of Carnegie Hall. Wow!

Recurrence happened one year after my chemo ended and I followed the same gold standard for treatment

CHAPTER 9: KAREN CONWAY

again. I lost my hair again, but I developed the attitude of, "Hey you did this once, you can do it again!" And lucky me, as a result of the ovarian cancer I developed Deep Vein Thromboses, which closed up some of the veins in my lower legs. It's a chronic disability, and nothing can be done to improve that. Hence my companion the cane.

Six months after my second diagnosis, I got my third hit: metastases to the brain. I opted for radiation and got zapped with all they had in just one session.

Repeated MRIs, CT and PET scans found my microscopic brain growth unchanged, yet kinda fuzzy. Had it grown? Had necrosis – tissue death – set in? Was it a reaction to the radiation?

More tests and finally a determination: it was tissue death from the radiation. And fortunately I had plenty of other brain tissue to make up for the dead stuff.

Finally some good news! The director of the church choir I sang with founded the Arizona Choral Society. Ahhh … choral masterworks. I was in heaven and I hadn't even died yet.

I eventually came to the conclusion that my cancer was a gift. It took me several years to admit that, and especially to say it out loud.

Not only have I made many incredible friendships, but I rediscovered my passion for music. Both have kept me alive all these many years later.

I fully understand that one can never return to what life was exactly like before cancer, but that's not so bad. We call it the "new normal," And "new normal" can apply to anyone in any situation. What have you always wanted to try but were afraid to tackle? What passion do you have that you want to rediscover, like I did with my music?

I'm here to tell you the sky's the limit – go for it!

CHAPTER **9**: **KAREN CONWAY**

PHOENIX

Spring in the desert is filled with magical sights and sounds. So it is with survivorship, as each of these Valley of the Sun women survivors found magic and miracles in the wake of the world's most dreaded disease. Their stories are testaments to a phrase often repeated by survivors: "Cancer was a gift."

Sunday, March 12, 2017, 2:00 p.m.
Mesa Arts Center, Mesa, AZ

This performance was made possible by the generosity of Cancer Treatment Centers of America, Scottsdale Medical Imaging, Ltd., Ironwood Cancer Research Center, Mosharrafa Plastic Surgery, and Kendra Scott Jewelry.

Love to Dave Pratt, Emcee, Founder of Star Worldwide Networks

CHAPTER 10

KARI GROVES
Thyroid Cancer Survivor

Kari is a native Arizonan, a wife, and the mother of two beautiful daughters. She serves as Program Man-ager for Singleton Moms, a local nonprofit organization dedicated to serving the needs of single parents battling cancer and their minor children. She embraces the organization's motto, "Meeting the needs of today and providing hope for tomorrow." Learn more at *www. singletonmoms.org.*

Papillary Thyroid Cancer – the "best cancer," they said, if you have to have cancer.

Picture this. It was 2004. I was 28 years old, a newly married wife and the mother of a two-year-old. On a Wednesday morning, I went into my doctor's office with a sore throat, where upon they found a lump the size of a golf ball. A biopsy followed on Friday, and I was immediately scheduled for the removal of my entire thyroid the following Monday. This would remove "the best cancer to have."

The surgery was effective, with only a couple of complications.

A month later, I received the I-131 radioactive iodine treatment which was prescribed to treat all the remaining nodules. This would completely eradicate "the best cancer to have."

Only it didn't. Over the course of the next four years, "the best cancer to have" came back, forcing me to endure three more excruciatingly difficult rounds of radiation treatment. Each one isolated me in a plastic lined hospital room resembling a giant Ziplock bag, for an entire week. I was kept from my daughter and any contact with my husband or family.

And then, after my third treatment, and against my doctor's orders, we got pregnant. We are now the proud parents of two amazingly beautiful daughters.

Apparently, I'll never be rid of "the best cancer to have." Since 2008, I have received regular six-month scans and oncology visits to watch the metastasis continue to grow. It happens at such a slow rate that removal isn't an option. And I've reached my lifetime limit of treatment of radioactive iodine treatments. Any more and I would likely contract leukemia.

So I wait, and plan for my family's future. But my cancer journey has allowed me to create an incredible 2nd Act!

In 2010, at the gentle and loving suggestion of my husband, I enrolled to get my Master's Degree in Nonprofit Management and Leadership. This in turn has allowed me to pursue greater and increasingly more meaningful and impactful work.

While living in Seattle, I became a Parents As Teachers Home Visitor with Friends of Youth. I mentored young, first time parents and their children to foster loving and educational relationships.

At the same time, I was also the Director of Children's Education at Bellevue First Congregational Church, designing and facilitating weekly teacher trainings, staff development and the loving education of our community's most vulnerable youth.

Life's journey is interesting, isn't it? Those work experiences, and having "the best cancer to have," prepared me for what has unfolded the last two years.

CHAPTER 10: KARI GROVES

In early 2015, without warning, our oldest daughter was struck over night with a debilitating and mysterious illness. It left our beautiful 13-year-old bed-ridden and in the fight for her life.

It started with persistent and unrelenting migraine-type headaches that continue to this day. She was diagnosed with Lyme's disease, which many physicians deem improbable and "fake."

Simultaneously she contracted fibromyalgia. Almost overnight, she lost the use of her limbs.

My husband and I, along with our entire family, each found our own methods of coping with her illness. But it was my first-hand cancer journey that guided me to process my daughter's situation in a unique and profound way.

Her illness brought our family closer than I ever thought possible. I'm happy to report she has improved immensely and is now functioning at almost 100%. And I have found yet another direction for my 2nd Act!

Incorporating my love for children and their families, along with "the best cancer to have," I am now the Program Manager for a local nonprofit organization called Singleton Moms. I lead a team of dedicated employees and volunteers, as we meet the families' needs of today and provide hope for their tomorrow.

CHAPTER 10: KARI GROVES

Eleven years ago, our founder, Jody Farley, helped a high school friend named Michelle Singleton.
Michelle was a single mom of four children when diagnosed with Stage IV breast cancer at a very young age.

After Michelle died, Jody recognized there had to be more parents in the Valley with Michelle's needs. Singleton Moms started on Jody's kitchen counter and now assists single parents battling cancer, and their minor children, throughout Maricopa County.

In my role, and using my personal experiences, I have had the incredible honor of honing programs that are uniquely structured for these families at their darkest time.

Our work is varied and vast. We partner with a local commercial kitchen called Dream Dinners to create 190 nutritious, gourmet and healthy meals for our families every month. Each meal is prepared by our volunteers.

And in coordination with Jody, I am spearheading a program for pediatric cancer patients and their families. This will include a support network for this unique population, all the while maintaining our core programs.

I am passionate about spreading our mission and our vision with community members, volunteers, donors and parents alike. Part of my 2nd Act is to make sure that we can gather and support as many families as

CHAPTER 10: KARI GROVES

possible. And being a part of this cast has magnified that potential. We even have a former Singleton Mom recipient in this cast!

Could I do this work simply with my degree? Probably. But would I be as effective and whole-heartedly compassionate without my own cancer journey? Doubtful.

Clearly "the best cancer to have" really has been!

CHAPTER **11**

NANCY LITTERMAN HOWE
Squamous Cell Cancer Survivor

Nancy was a daily exerciser who ate her fruits and vegetables. But in 1997, she was diagnosed with cancer anyway. She experienced first-hand the benefits of physical activity during treatment and beyond. That was her "Aha!" moment. She left her corporate career, returned to school, and founded *www. StrongCancerRecovery.org*.

CHAPTER **11:** NANCY LITTERMAN HOWE

Hello! I am definitely the vaudeville portion of today's program. Let me explain how I came to be on the stage today.

In 2013 I created my 2nd Act when I founded my non-profit, Strong Cancer Recovery. I have one focus: advocate for exercise to become part of the Standard of Care for oncology treatment.

I believed then, and I believe even more strongly now, that change will come when cancer patients loudly request exercise programs from their oncologists, and oncologists press their administrators for in-house exercise facilities for their patients.

Part of my work is to speak at cancer-related events, where I describe my own cancer diagnosis and treatment, and the research-proven benefits of exercise for people living with a diagnosis of cancer. I distribute resistance bands and teach exercises too.

In 2015, I spoke at a dozen events, reaching nearly 800 survivors and oncologists. But I wanted to reach more. A year ago, I learned of an opportunity for me to reach nearly 900 seniors in a single night. All I needed to do was enter the Ms. Senior Arizona pageant, and turn my 20-minute advocacy talk into a two-and-a-half-minute talent.

Which I did.

So while the other 20 contestants were dressed in elegant gowns and singing, or wearing top hats and tails as they tap-danced, I took the stage, dressed like this, and explained the benefits of exercise for cancer survivorship to the full auditorium of 925!

Although my talent was highly unconventional, the judges clearly got it. Like me, they saw the value in my message being delivered to as many seniors as possible. I placed third overall, and during that one week, I spoke to more than 1100 seniors in Phoenix's West Valley.

I know that the groundswell demand from patients for structured exercise programs will continue to grow.
It is my hope that, as a group, oncologists will make time during clinical visits to emphasize to their patients the importance of physical activity.

Research suggests that patients are twice as likely to start exercising if their oncologist recommends it. We're not re-creating the wheel here. We just need to get it rolling!

These days, when I speak, I remind oncologists that it doesn't take much time or a deep knowledge of exercise physiology to make this recommendation.

In fact, my two-and-a-half minute talent at the Ms. Senior Arizona Contest is exactly what I want oncologists to promote.

CHAPTER **11: NANCY LITTERMAN HOWE**

My passion is teaching magic. Let me tell you why.

In 1997 I was 42, a daily exerciser, and I ate my fruits and vegetables. I got cancer anyway.

It was aggressive – a rapidly growing, golf-ball-sized tumor in my throat. Treatment was aggressive too, and exhausting, with gruesome side effects.

My surgery removed the roof of my mouth, creating a cavernous echo chamber for my voice.

The radiation dried up my salivary glands. Let me assure you that saliva is a very under-rated body fluid. For the first three years following treatment, my meal plans included protein shakes, oatmeal, and ice-cream. Not all bad!

But back then, they couldn't target radiation like they can now, so my head and neck radiation was also carotid artery and heart radiation, for which I see a cardiac specialist, despite my active lifestyle.

I could also tell you about the disastrous effects on my teeth – again no saliva – which cost about the same as a Mercedes convertible, and not nearly as much fun.

But when I came through far better than expected, my oncologist guessed it was because I was so fit when we started treatment.

My diagnosis, and strong recovery, gave me a mission.

At 51, I earned my master's degree in exercise at Arizona State University. And today, 11 years later, I work with the oncology team at Mayo Clinic.

I teach cancer patients that exercise reduces their risk of relapse, lessens the long-term side effects of treatment, and combats depression.

Most of my patients are 50 and older. Most already feel terrible about themselves for not exercising enough. That's when I teach them the magic of exercise.

You see, the benefits of exercise are cumulative. Even if we can only exercise for two minutes before we have to stop and rest. I point out that two minutes every hour in an eight hour day is 16 minutes of exercise. And 16 minutes is more than half of the 30 minutes recommended by the Surgeon General.

That's success! That feels like magic!

So what do we do for two minutes that makes such a difference?

We sit down, and we stand up. We sit down, we stand up, we sit down, we stand UP.

And how much do we do? More than the day before. And really, that's all that's needed to trigger the benefits of exercise for anybody.

So I ask you, "Isn't that a kind of magic?"

CHAPTER **11: NANCY LITTERMAN HOWE**

But there's more to my 2nd Act. Last month, I was hired by Arizona State University to research the very subject I've been so passionate about.

As a Research Specialist Senior, I'll be able to truly contribute to the science I've long known improves and saves lives.

Now that's magic!

CHAPTER 12

SUE ELLEN ALLEN
Breast Cancer Survivor

Sue Ellen Allen is an activist, speaker and author whose remarkable journey through cancer introduced her to a life's purpose that took her to the White House. She is the founder of *www.ReinventingReentry.org* and the author of *The Slumber Party From Hell*, a memoir of turning tragedy to triumph.

CHAPTER **12:** SUE ELLEN ALLEN

Valentine's Day, 2002, I was diagnosed with stage 3B breast cancer. My prognosis was less than five years. My treatment would be chemotherapy, followed by surgery.

Then suddenly, that July, humiliated and disgraced, I entered the Maricopa County jail to await sentencing for securities fraud.

I went to my mastectomy shackled, handcuffed and belly chained. No friends or family present. No one touched me but the surgeons with their knives, the nurses with their needles and the guards with their handcuffs.

I'd lost 28 lymph nodes along with my breast and the surgeon issued an order to the jail for a pillow to cushion and protect my arm from lymphedema.
Order denied. No pillows were allowed in the jail.

When I got back from the hospital, women packed into my cell to see how I was. Breaking a huge rule, they hugged me, the first hugs I'd received. Aren't hugs wonderful?

These tough women were so upset about the pillow rule, they left my cell grumbling. A few hours later they were back with an order of their own. "Close your eyes, Sue Ellen, and hold out your hands."

When I did, I felt the softest thing: it was the most

beautiful pillow I have ever seen, light blue, tufted and fringed, and it did not come in a Tiffany bag.

Where on earth? Then I realized it was made of the Kotex pads furnished by the jail! These tough women had contributed their precious supplies and woven them together into a tufted square.

They used the small golf pencil that's allowed for a writing tool to punch holes in the ends of the pads. They shredded thin strips from another pad to use as thread to sew it all around. Finally, they fringed it to give it that designer look.

At the darkest time in my life, drug addicts, prostitutes, and murderers looked after me, and I will NEVER forget them.

March 18, 2009, I was finally free. I started working in the criminal justice system because I found my purpose and my 2nd Act in prison. In eight years I've worked to bring education inside the women's prison. And I've worked to bring education outside to the general public, by drawing attention to the horror of our prison system, especially if you're sick.

I watched my cell mate die of leukemia because the prison kept denying her a simple blood test.

She was so sick and when they finally took her to the hospital, her red blood count was 300,000 and her white blood count was ZERO.

CHAPTER **12:** SUE ELLEN ALLEN

I'd never seen a body shut down. The pain was excruciating. Gina was only 25. Her three year sentence became a death sentence.

After her death, I asked if we could have a cancer walk in October. I didn't know it had NEVER been done before. The prison staff looked at me like I had three heads, but they finally agreed.

We decorated the yard with pink construction paper – the place looked like a Pepto Bismol explosion!   We walked around and around the track, and raised $10,000 from inmates and staff for the American Cancer Society. That was in 2003 and that walk is still going on in Arizona prisons, raising money for cancer.

If you had told me before I went to prison what I'd see and experience, I would have said, "Not in our country. We don't treat people that way." I was wrong. We do, and being sick is especially terrifying.

So my 2nd Act is to educate the public about this draconian $80 billion business.   America is the incarceration nation, incarcerating more people per capita than Russia or China.

In prison, I encountered a lot of single mothers, there because of addiction. Their children were being raised by others. In America, 1 in 28 children now has a parent in prison. In America, every 26 seconds, a child drops out of school. In America, one in three people has a criminal record. How is that acceptable in America?

January 3, 2016, seven years after I was freed. I was waiting for Downton Abby to start. My phone rang. ID unknown. I don't answer ID unknown. Rang again. Ignored it. Rang AGAIN. This time voice mail. OK, I'll listen.

"Ms. Allen, this is XYZ at the White House calling. Would you please call me back as soon as possible?"

Oh sure, the White House calling ME. I don't think so. Did you know you can Google the White House? Nice operators 24/7. So I called just to verify it wasn't a hoax. I gave them the name left on my voice mail. "Yes ma'm, that's one of our staffers." OK, I thought. I guess I'd better call back.

The call was an invitation to be one of 23 Americans to sit in the First Lady's box at President Obama's final State of the Union address. I was to represent criminal justice reform. I was very cool.

"You know I'm an ex-felon?" "Yes, ma'am, we know all about you."

A week later I was on a whirlwind trip to Washington, D.C., where I was interviewed by NBC in front of the White House and the BBC on the radio. I met with the Attorney General Loretta Lynch. Me, a former inmate. I attended a gorgeous reception at the White House. It

CHAPTER **12: SUE ELLEN ALLEN**

seemed more like a movie than real life.

I met Mrs. Obama and Dr. Biden, then rode in a motorcade to the capitol, sirens blazing.

Looking down from the First Lady's box in the historic chamber of the House of Representatives, I could see all of our Congressional leaders, the Supreme Court Justices, the Cabinet and Joint Chiefs of Staff. Just like on TV.

Then in a flash it was over. Our security detail came to escort us, I thought, to the motorcade back to the White House. But instead, they took us into a long hallway where we waited and waited.

Finally, I asked why. "Don't you know, Sue Ellen?" came the response from another person who'd been in the box with me. "We're going to meet the President and have our picture taken!"

Oh my goodness. My first thought was pure vanity: my lipstick is in my purse, in the limousine in the motorcade!

We inched up to the door and then it was my turn. There stood the President.

He beamed and gave me a huge hug and I thanked him for visiting a prison last summer. We had a brief chat then he turned me just right to make sure the picture was perfect. And it was.

CHAPTER **12:** SUE ELLEN ALLEN

In June of last year, I was invited back to speak on a panel on criminal justice at a White House sponsored summit, "The United State of Women."

In November, I went back one more time to speak to a group of leaders in justice reform. Led by the Attorney General and Presidential Advisor Valerie Jarrett, their message inspired us to continue our work and never give up on our purpose and our vision.

Do you make New Year's resolutions or set goals. I don't, but if I did, never EVER would I have set a goal that one day I would be in the First Lady's box at the State of the Union in our nation's Capitol. That's like saying, I'm going to win an Oscar without ever being in a movie!

It's what I call God's magic. It's the reason we can never give up. Life can change in an instant to terrify you, like when you hear the words, "You've got cancer." It can also change instantly to thrill you. Like when the White House calls and the result gives your 2nd Act the kind of power and attention it deserves. It's God's magic.

I ask you ALL to remember God's magic and God's message that after cancer and often because of cancer, there is life and purpose and passion.

ALL of these women here are examples that cancer can give us the power to grow stronger so we can Show Up, Speak Up and Do Stuff in our 2nd Act!

CHAPTER **12:** SUE ELLEN ALLEN

CHAPTER **13**

NADIA J. SAMUEL
Hodgkin's Lymphoma
Cancer Survivor

Nadia is certified in Cancer Peer Support through Arizona Cancer Survivors Circle of Strength, a community of cancer survivors and advocates who provide support to those touched by cancer. She is also an advocate for stress elimination through balance and meditation. As an entrepreneur, she has developed Stress Nano, which offers solutions anyone can achieve.

Learn more at *www.StressNano.com.*

We all have a story, and it can be told in many ways -- through social media ... via frames lining the walls of our childhood bedrooms ... in the faces and expressions of the ones you count on as your support team or confidants ... or in a medical report.

Today I will try to capture my story for you, if only just for a few moments.

My 2nd Act began in 2007, when I became cancer free. This year marks my 10 year anniversary!

Within my 2nd Act, I feel I was gifted a new chance to discover my path, truly identifying who I am, helping to redefine my story, discerning which dreams belong solely to me, and to chase them to their end or until they weave themselves into reality.

And I realized you can have thousands of dreams! I do – and each one is unique and beautiful.

My cancer diagnosis came as a complete surprise. I mean, it's almost always a surprise to those of us who have been diagnosed. I had just turned 21. Woo - hoo! I was officially an adult.

On a quick visit home from college – for Mom's express laundry service and such – I found my mother in the kitchen. She looked at me and said, "Wow, you look horrible!"

Thanks, Mom.

"No really you should see a doctor," she said. The "I've-been-busy-and-I-have-a-lot-of-pressure-at-school" responses didn't quell her pushing. So I went the next day and came home with a smug smile.

"I just need to eat breakfast and take more vitamins."
"Go see another doctor," my mother said.

Within 20 minutes into the exam with my new doctor – the one I chose out of the insurance book, with the most abbreviations next to her name, to keep my mom quiet – she said, "You have cancer. Cancel classes and let's get you to an oncologist right away."

Confirmed by five different oncologists, I had had Hodgkin's Lymphoma for two years already. I was at stage II, and tumors had begun to expand in two separate systems in my body.

Choosing a treatment plan and the right oncologist took much longer than diagnosis. The difficulty was due to the fact that I was a bit of a puzzle. Half of the doctors specialized in treating much older patients and the other half specialized in pediatrics.

Treatment protocols for each group varied considerably. Sitting in each waiting room, I felt out of place. I either stared at toys on the floor, or retirement ads while the doctors contemplated factors they usually didn't, like fertility or college classes. In the end, they tossed me into the pediatric group. There went my official adult pass!

CHAPTER **13:** NADIA J. SAMUEL

There were some bumps during chemo. And with no support group for my age group, I was thankful and fortunate to have chosen an oncology team that truly understood my frustration at this juncture. They gave me a voice during treatment, and a special place of my own in their office.

After the flurry of treatment I navigated my new path in my 2nd Act, two main dreams became clearer and clearer as I grew into my new skin. Both had the same mission: to always reach out to those who need, to give them a hand as they make their way through their own stories.

The first dream, was to become a volunteer and peer support advocate for cancer patients and survivors.

As a volunteer, I hoped to contribute my stories, my mistakes, my tips and above all, hope.

And though I wished to help as many as possible, my passion was to gain as much experience as I could as a Peer Advocate. I wanted to help those who found themselves wedged in the generational gap, between pediatrics and a much older generation.

It is hard to believe that 10 years later, though treatment and access to information are dramatically enhanced, support for the young adult group – from a perspective they can relate to – has not improved much.

I was so ecstatic to find Arizona Cancer Survivors Circle of Strength, a volunteer community of cancer survivors, caregivers, friends and families who provide hope, strength, and support to those who have been touched by cancer.

This group has welcomed me with open arms, allowing me to explore this pursuit and I am truly grateful. They have given me the opportunity to obtain my Peer Support Certification as I embarked on my 2nd Act.

I support them by volunteering at events, runs and walks put on by partner organizations in our community. I am also excited to assist Circle of Strength with social media outreach and interaction within our community. I have joined their fundraising committee for 2017 and am writing exclusive pieces for their blog.

The board at Circle of Strength has been extremely supportive in my personal passion.

And with their guidance, I will pursue this dream until everyone in the young adult age group, whether patient or survivor, can say they have a fount of support that focuses on their needs.

My other 2nd Act mission focuses on a serious chronic illness that plagues millions of Americans every day, one for which it's hard to find help: chronic stress.

Yes, it is a lofty goal, but I believe with the right

CHAPTER **13:** NADIA J. SAMUEL

support, we can all achieve a healthy state of balance, where our physical, mental, and emotional health are not plagued by daily recurrent, constant stress.

This dream has stemmed from my cancer experience.

Through cancer survivorship, I have witnessed the power of a support team, those who will go the extra mile to research alternative medicine, statistics on current treatments, and any clinical trials necessary to eliminate the disease so the patient can resume the life they were meant to have.

I believe that we should apply the same gusto and diligence toward eliminating stress. It can wreak havoc on our bodies, and in addition to mental health and emotional stability, it has even been linked to cancer.

From this passion, I created Stress Nano. I have assembled an expert team to develop a website and an app which will become a custom support team.

We are assembling every useful stress elimination method. They are intended to be a continuous solution, not simply a temporary state. We call this "stress release," instead of stress relief. When we feel relief, we're getting a temporary reprieve, but eventually the main source of the problem will rear its head. And then we seek temporary relief again and the cycle continues.

Our custom algorithm helps each user define the best

course of action in stress release suited to their profile.

Through a series of questions developed by specialists in psychology, yoga, massage therapy, education, meditation, nutrition, breath-work and mindfulness, users are able to get to the root of their stress. They can bypass solutions that may not be the most effective for them, and begin the release process immediately.

Users can also enhance their profiles and suggested solutions by entering or seamlessly integrating data from wireless devices such as heart rate monitors, fitness devices and even playlists!

This beloved project of mine will launch later this year. It combines so many things I love and find important: self-care, meditation, mindfulness, and other modalities. And it is an incredibly important agent in the fight against cancer.

So this is my 2nd Act. I will continuously strive to help as many as I can from as many perspectives that are available to me. I will dream for as long as I have this gift.

And my story will continue to be written.

CHAPTER **14**

REBA MASON
Breast Cancer Survivor

This Texas girl lives in Surprise, AZ, and is the Founder and CEO of Reba's Vision. The organization provides free 3D digital mammograms to Phoenix area women, as well as wigs, prosthetics and bras free of charge to any woman in need while they are going through their cancer battle. Learn more at *www.RebasVision.com.*

CHAPTER **14:** REBA MASON

My life has been filled with ups and downs, from being a Dallas Cowboys Cheerleader for four seasons, to battling an eating disorder that nearly took my life in 2000 and successfully overcoming it.

For my 40th birthday, my mom had given me the unique present of being tested to see if I carried the BRCA gene mutation. My grandmother, my mom, her twin sister, two cousins, and two other relatives had been diagnosed with either breast or ovarian cancer. Not surprisingly, I, too, carry the BRCA ER positive 2 gene mutation.

And then, on October 1, 2011, for better or worse, my first act ended for good. I had gone in for my six month mammogram. The doctor called and told me I needed to come in right away. I knew I had breast cancer, and indeed it was. They first thought it would be stage one. But in surgery, they discovered it was far more advanced. I had stage 3c invasive ductal carcinoma and awoke with a double mastectomy.

I knew this would forever change my life. My treatment was tough – 16 weeks of chemo, followed by 32 rounds of radiation. When that didn't work, the process was repeated. And then it was repeated again, for a total of 48 weeks of chemo and 96 rounds of radiation. Whew!

My chemo port became infected and was replaced three times, more cancer was discovered and I underwent surgery after surgery. But I knew I had to fight like a girl! And that became my motto.

At the same time, my mom, Marla Sue Mason, was battling stage 4 metastatic breast cancer. She had been fighting for 18 years and it came back four times, but she never gave up.

She volunteered at the center where she was receiving treatment and would tell everyone, "I don't have a terminal illness. I have a chronic illness that can be managed with treatment and faith." She fought like a girl, too, until she lost her battle on February 24, 2014.

Seven months later, in September of 2014, my life would begin its 2nd Act.

My amazing doctors informed me that my cancer had metastasized to my bones. My life expectancy was two to four years, maybe. Yes, I had my "why me" pity party that night. But at 2:00 a.m., I woke up, realizing I had had two visions.

Three weeks earlier, I had heard about a new type of mammogram, 3D digital tomography. It was reducing call-backs by 40%, and catching breast cancer up to 18 months earlier than a normal 2D mammogram.

I also learned that, without insurance, it cost a woman $111 to have this latest, more effective mammogram. I stared writing down cost times this, times that, and Reba's Vision was born!
If I could raise $3,000, I could maybe save 25 women

CHAPTER **14:** **REBA MASON**

from what I and so many others have gone through.

I also wanted to help women currently in treatment feel beautiful. And this was the second vision. I began providing them with a Basket of Hope. These baskets come from their surrounding community, and are filled with books, hats, makeup, jewelry, and anything else that gives them hope.

I had been given such items while I was undergoing my treatment. Little did I imagine that two years later, we would have raised nearly $100,000!

At the time, I was the marketing director at a Texas Roadhouse Restaurant, and the managing partner allowed me to turn the restaurant pink for the month of October. Over 100 women have used the Pink Roadhouse Mammo Fund.

In addition, Reba's Vision has provided more than 75 Hope Baskets.

My 2nd Act continues to grow as we now provide free wigs, bras, prosthetics, hats, scarves, anything a woman needs while in treatment for any form of cancer. It's all at no cost to them, through the generous donations from women who have been there and survived.

My 2nd Act is still going strong with the amazing support of my husband, who I met while battling cancer and married 11 months ago, and includes my family and countless friends, especially Gina Sheets.

CHAPTER **14: REBA MASON**

I'm ready to begin my 3rd Act now. I will not let a little thing called cancer beat me. Because I know how to fight like a girl!

CHAPTER 15

JAN COGGINS
Ovarian Cancer Survivor

Jan is a survivor, educator, spiritual leader, and the author of *Ovarian Cancer? You Can Not Be Serious!* A retired social worker who passionately advocates for ovarian cancer awareness, Jan's own cancer jour-ney keeps her motivated to find funds and resources for women with ovarian cancer through her organization the Teal It Up Foundation. Learn more at *www. TealItUp.org.*

CHAPTER **15:** JAN COGGINS

Don't tell God the size of the mountain, tell the mountain the size of God.

Eight months after chemo for stage 3C ovarian cancer, and in celebration of my 60th birthday, I hiked 100 miles in the Swiss Alps. My gynecological oncologist said that I might be a little crazy when I told him I was hiking. But I did it anyway.

With neuropathy, it wasn't pretty. But along with my team of supporters, we made it. After that success, I got serious about survivorship.

Looking back over some of the cliffs I crossed in the Alps, I probably should have given some thought to survivorship then. But my mindset was that I had beaten cancer, and the mountains were next.

I am a seven-year survivor and thriver of ovarian cancer. And I consider that a feat greater than the mountain climbing. I live grate-FULL every day for life after such a diagnosis. Especially since I have lost more friends to this disease than I can bear to share.

It's been though faith, will, strength and the desire to help another person face this kind of adversity that I have found my way.

So many people had helped me during my journey that I wanted to give back. Every time I saw someone I thought might be in treatment, I'd approach them. And

CHAPTER **15:** JAN COGGINS

before you knew it, we had a wonderful connection.

I felt like I could be a lightning rod to change the way they looked at their cancer. I told them to have the attitude of "Yes, I have cancer, but it doesn't have me;" "I am full of life, not cancer;" "See me, not it." I rocked the attitude that I would beat cancer and I want every other cancer patient to do the same.

My recurrence in 2012 hit hard, because I was so into rocking my survivorship. It took every fiber of my soul to stay on track and not go down the proverbial black hole.

Before my recurrence, I had begun writing a book entitled "Ovarian Cancer: You Can Not Be Serious!" It was launched in the spring of 2013, while I was still in chemo. And to my amazement, the book has been successful. I continue to receive emails from women across the country.

But I wanted to do more. So I formed the Teal It Up Foundation. Now, starting a foundation is sort of like hiking the Alps – crazy! But we have reached thousands, and given over $100,000 toward research for a cure to ovarian cancer.

Losing board members to the disease has been hugely impactful on me and the other board members. So in the past year, we decided to keep our funds local to help women within Arizona. We offer comfort bags to newly diagnosed and recurring gynecological cancer

CHAPTER **15:** JAN COGGINS

patients.

But one of the most rewarding programs we've started is our pet therapy program. Please meet Bozeman.

He was certified at the age of one to visit chemo rooms and hospitals by referral. Bozeman moves from patient to patient, hanging out with them and always near enough for them to love on him. The patients are held captive by their chemo lines. But he brings them such joy that his visits are highly requested.

If I could bottle the joy he brings to me and others, well ... suffice it to say, I'd be in the Caribbean right now!

He's as much a part of my continued healing and well being as he is to those he meets during his day job.

But there's something else I'm as passionate about as Bozeman – genetic testing. There was no cancer in my family and in 2012, when I was BRCA tested, I was negative for the mutation. But new gene mutations were discovered and I was retested in 2015.

This time, I was positive for the PALB 2 mutation, which puts me at higher risk for pancreatic, breast and ovarian cancers. And here's the kicker. Both my sisters were tested and they're both positive as well.

Why am I telling you this? Genetic research and testing can mean the difference between life and death for many. So the Teal It Up Foundation funds anyone unable to pay for testing, if it's been deemed medically indicated. Some of the women we've helped have been found positive. I know those test results made a difference in their treatment options.

Now I'm not a public speaker. I grew up a terrible stutterer, so I'm about done here, because things could go south at any moment.

But I believe in helping people understand that they are a big part in helping themselves, no matter what cancer, what stage, what age.

The C-word is dreaded and for good reason. But I have chosen to focus on the opening in the letter C. Each and every day, I welcome the blessings and opportunities that flow into the opening, that they may be a part of my plan to impact for the greater good.

My goal is to see myself as whole, and to pass something worthwhile to others. I firmly believe blessings can come from any adversity that we face.

As a certified spiritual director, I believe we are all here to shepherd one another on our spiritual journeys.

Let me close with a quote from Pierre Teilhard de Chardin: "We are not human beings having a spiritual experience. We are spiritual beings having a human experience." Welcome to your experience!

CHAPTER **15:** JAN COGGINS

CHAPTER 16

ELIZABETH CAMERON
Ewing's Cancer Survivor

This "one hip wonder" is a 15-year-old cancer survivor making a difference in her community and around the world. Elizabeth is an advocate for childhood cancer, speaking and volunteering with many organiza-tions. She creates makeup bags for girls in the hospital who are going through treatment, as well as providing them with Positivity Pouches. Learn more about her at *www.LittleGoldWarrior.com.*

CHAPTER **16:** ELIZABETH CAMERON

Hi, my name is Elizabeth. If you can't tell I'm a little bit on the short side, 4' 7" to be exact, and that's just on my good leg. My dad is 6' 2" and my mom is five feet. She hoped my dad's genes would help her kids be taller. I'm short and my brother was born with dwarfism. It kinda back fired on her.

Around Easter of 2015, I woke up with a slight pain in my leg. At first, I thought to myself, it's a growing pain! I'm finally growing! The pain got worse and I just figured that it was a dance pain. I've been a dancer since I was two, so injuries were bound to happen.

The pain went away but then it returned. And this time, it was so intense that I could no longer walk or do anything. It became so bad that my parents took me to the doctor to get an x-ray. The x-ray showed nothing, so the doctor referred me to physical therapy. After a few sessions, the pain became worse still. The next diagnosis was a problem with my hip flexor.

The physical therapist said he had never seen a hip flexor so tight in someone so young and he recommended I get an MRI. Bad news: the MRI came back showing an egg-sized mass in my hip. They said it could be lymphoma, sarcoma or leukemia.

We then met with the surgeon who assured us it was more than likely a benign tumor and off I went for a biopsy.

CHAPTER **16:** ELIZABETH CAMERON

He said he would call my parents in a week once he received the results.

During that time, I was in a tremendous amount of pain but we remained positive and convinced ourselves it was benign. So I named the tumor "Bean" for benign.

A week later, my dad received a phone call, not from the surgeon, but from Phoenix Children's Cancer and Blood Center. They told him my tumor was malignant. There goes the name "Bean!"

We met with an oncologist and she told me that I had a rare bone cancer called Ewing's Sarcoma.

She told me I would have nine months of chemotherapy, surgery and possibly radiation. I told the oncologist that I didn't have time to deal with this, and that I would give her three months.

She disagreed, but I didn't let that get me down. I was admitted that day, July 6th, 2015, and that was the start of my roller coaster.

After the first six rounds of chemo, I had a 12-hour surgery, which resulted in the removal of my entire left hip with no replacement. Joint replacements can sometimes cause infections – which I did not need! In addition, I'm hopefully still growing and a hip today may not fit me tomorrow!

I was told I would not be able to dance or do a lot of

other things again. I took this as a challenge.

I've always been the type of person who, when you tell me one thing, I most likely will wanna do the opposite. I might have been a little bit of challenging child at times.

I'm sure most people hadn't seen a one hip dancer. I mean, a one hip anything sounds a little weird. I was going to prove them wrong and I did. I may not dance like I used to, but I dance!

I now call myself the "One Hip Wonder." My left leg is three and a half inches shorter than my right, so I have to wear a shoe lift. Its okay because I've accepted it and it's now my friend.

It was a hard 12 months. I spent over 150 nights in the hospital, multiple hours of physical therapy, countless days of being wheeled around the hospital campus from doctor appointment to doctor appointment. There were hours of throwing up, sleepless nights, anxiety, shots, nasty medicine, pain and ER visits.

If you can imagine being sick all the time, then you can understand it wasn't very fun. But I still woke up every morning and told myself, it's okay. There's someone somewhere who has it so much worse than you do. Be thankful that you woke up this morning and are still breathing.

I'm a strong believer that everything happens for a

reason. I knew that I had to go through that so that now I can live out my 2nd Act. And I would go through it all over again because from this, I've gained so much perspective and found so many opportunities to make a difference and learn.

I learned that childhood cancer is a very big problem that no one knows about unless you are in this world. I learned that 47 kids are diagnosed every single day, and seven more become angels every day. Not because of their unwillingness to fight this horrible disease, but because there are no more options for them.

Less than 4 percent of federal funding goes to childhood cancer and that's not okay! We are given a harsh chemo regimen that destroys our immune systems and has many long term side effects.

We lose our hair, our eyebrows and our eyelashes. We are either in the hospital or at home sick. No one sees us. There is not enough awareness for childhood cancer.

Since finding out these facts, I have made it my mission to do whatever I can to make a difference and I've only just begun. Makeup was my therapy during treatment. I would tell people, okay no one bother me. I'm worrying about my face right now and that's all.

It was a distraction from how I was feeling and whatever else was going on in my life. It also made me feel better. I mean, I may not have felt good but I

CHAPTER **16:** ELIZABETH CAMERON

looked good! I wanted to give that feeling to others, so I decided to give girls in the hospital all the tools they would need and it would be great.

I have started to create personalized makeup bags for teen girls in local hospitals. My goal is to expand this to hospitals nationwide. I have already started connecting with other organizations to help make this possible.

I have also spoken at several events, sharing my story and spreading awareness about childhood cancer issues.

Another project in my 2nd Act is creating "Personalized Positivity Pouches" with my aunt. These are special IV pole covers that have pouches on the outside to store positive messages. That way, positivity is covering all of your medicines and chemo bags.

I feel this this is important because we need to think that everything going into our bodies is healing. I had a chemo called the "red devil" because it's red and does the most damage to your heart. It comes in a black bag that says, "Caution, hazardous material."

This can scary to little kids, so having a Personalized Positivity Pouch helps them not think about it. I believe that thinking positive thoughts is very powerful.

On my Facebook fan page, I'm the Little Gold Warrior. Obviously, I'm little. Gold is the color of childhood cancer. And I am a warrior.

Look out world, this Little Gold Warrior's 2nd Act has just begun and I plan to do big things!

CHAPTER **16:** ELIZABETH CAMERON

CHAPTER **17**

ELANA K. WIGHT
Ovarian Cancer Survivor

Elana is a sixth generation Arizona native and single mother of two high school students. In 2013, she was diagnosed with Stage IV Metastatic Ovarian Cancer. She founded the Red Thursday Foundation, and is also a speaker and business consultant for the professional beauty industry, reaching out to cancer pa-tients and beauty professionals throughout the world.

Learn more at *www.RedThursday.org*.

CHAPTER **17:** ELANA K. WIGHT

Elana Kathryn Wight, and I am a warrior!

On December 12, 2013, after four months of countless doctors visits, my worst fears came true. I had cancer. Not just any cancer but Stage IV Ovarian Cancer. I begin to scream inside.

How can this be? I'm 35. I'm young and vibrant. I'm healthy. I look good! I'm the fun one! This is not me. This isn't happening to me. Cancer happens to "those people." Not me.

What happens to my kids? I'm a single mom. They need me. I've got stuff to do. I have people who depend on me.

Frozen. All I feel is frozen.

Have you ever watched someone with end staged cancer? That's not me. That's not how this goes. That's not my life.

With God's help, I decided to write my own story that day. It would be my personal warrior journey, my mantra about life and not about cancer.

I pulled on my red cowboy boots. I put on my red lipstick, and I went to work: ready to live! I made a conscious choice to share all the details of this journey on social media. I shared my gory, scary, sad and triumphant moments with the world.

I was writing almost every day about my new zeal to live. I decided that each day I had the opportunity to be a better person than the day before, and if it mattered to just one person, then it was worth it.

Chemo after surgery, after surgery after chemo. And brain tumors after brain strokes, and then radiation after surgery after chemo and then more radiation. Drug trials after more chemo, and three times it came back.

Are you listening? It's more than I can explain and more than anyone should endure. But my red boots are still on. I'm smiling with my red lipstick on my lips and I'm still writing my story.

Today I am cancer free.

My red boots and red lipstick helped mold my 2nd Act. When I went through treatment the first time, I had chemo every week on Thursday. I wore my red cowboy boots and put on my red lipstick.

My friends came to chemo with me. We started sharing our weekly pictures of our chemo parties on Facebook and people began to notice. We were having fun! Imagine that? Who has fun at chemo? I do!

And it happened. More people joined me and started wearing red each Thursday.

They posted their own photos to show support to me

and to other cancer patients in their lives. We were seeing posts from all over the world. People noticed life. Thursday became the day to celebrate life, friendship and love.

Red was the color, not because I chose it, but because of all the different emotions it evokes: love, anger, beauty, and courage. Even Ulta Beauty would sell out of "F-Bomb" red lipstick! People loved it, this movement of ours.

My tiny spark became the fire that is now Red Thursday. It went from a social media movement to a small tribe of friends, and last year, only two and half years into this warrior's journey, I was able to create the Red Thursday Foundation.

It is my life's work, my 2nd Act and the divine purpose that God created me to do. I'm reaching as many cancer patients as possible and sharing my warrior journey.

Last year the Red Thursday Foundation hit several milestones. For my 38th birthday, April 28th we delivered red roses to over 300 cancer patients receiving treatment that day.

It was my birthday wish to celebrate life with as many patients as possible. Then, on September 29th, we had our first fundraising gala event.

Last year, I counseled over 250 cancer patients who

reached out to me personally. I have held more hands during chemo than I can count. I cry with them and then I make then laugh by being me, the crazy red head.

We are all in this together. We deliver food and supplies to anyone who asks. I'll talk to anyone who needs us. Our mission is to encourage, inspire and share hope for cancer patients and their caregivers. We believe Red Thursday can be celebrated by everyone, because today, everyone knows someone with cancer.

2017 is going to be an epic year for the Red Thursday Foundation. My goal for Red Thursday is to be used however we can for the advocacy of cancer patients in Arizona.

Last month on Valentine's Day, we delivered marula oil lip balms, specially packaged with our contact info on them so those patients can reach out to us for help in their journey. Our goal is to deliver another 20,000 throughout 2017. Twenty thousand lips is 20,000 happy hearts with hope. And hope saves lives.

I hope to personally make contact with at least half of those patients. I also look for other service opportunities where Red Thursday can partner with organizations to aid them for the support of patients.

There is one more gift cancer brought me. Beyond my 2nd Act, and the crazy red head is Elana. For the first time in my life, I can say I really like her. I am proud to

CHAPTER **17:** ELANA K. WIGHT

be her. I want to be her friend. She is exactly what the Lord created her to be, and she will never stop living!

TUCSON

There is a Native American saying: "If you're not living on the edge, you're taking up too much room."

You are about to learn the stories of eight women survivors of ALL cancers who are certainly living on the edge. Their cancer diagnosis didn't beat them, it made them more powerful and more HUMAN. They are true blessings in the world.

Sunday, November 5, 2017, 2:00 p.m
Berger Center for the Performing Arts, Tucson, AZ

This performance was made possible by the generosity of Radiation Ltd., Printex, Homewood Suites/St. Phillip's Plaza, KVOA and MIXfm.

Love to Mrs. Grant, Emcee
MIXfm Morning Mix

CHAPTER **18:** JEAN THOMAS

CHAPTER 18

JEAN THOMAS
Breast, Uterine, & Ovarian Cancer Survivor

Jean is a passionate volunteer for Buenos Aires Nation Wildlife Refuge, having led 135 guided, interpretive four-mile hikes in the Baboquivari Mountain's Brown Canyon. That's 135 and still counting, now as a septuagenarian! For 15 years, she was a Reach-to-Recovery volunteer and supports and mentors cancer survivors with Tucson Cancer Conquerors. Learn more about at Buenos Aires Nation Wildlife Refuge *www.fws.gov/refuge/buenos_aires/*

I'm in my 6th Act or so, depending upon whether you count those two little old skin cancers! I have the BRCA1 gene mutation, so in 1974, at age 34 — ta-da — I had breast cancer. I had another breast cancer in 2001, and uterine and ovarian cancers in 2005.

I'm 77. But my 82-year-old second cousin has had seven types of cancer as opposed to my lowly six. Apparently we're having a race and she's winning at present.

Soon after my first mastectomy in Ames, Iowa, an American Cancer Society volunteer came to our door.

Without a word, our son Tim, who was 8 at the time, ran upstairs to his room and brought down his glass piggy bank. He emptied it to "help cure cancer," as he put it.

The 2001 Her2 Neu positive breast cancer was really tough, and required as much chemo and radiation as I could handle. At one point my oncologist wanted to cut the chemo dose. But I said, "I want the max — I want to LIVE." The doc replied, "Well Jean, we have to keep you alive to live!"

Each Friday, after my chemo, I was wheeled to the hospital next door to spend the weekends receiving IV fluids, steroids, and anti-nausea meds.

If I took those anti-nausea meds orally, the pills would

simply bounce right back up. I was very ill through that nine-month ordeal.

After the weekend of IVs, my oncologist would bound into my hospital room on Monday mornings, saying, "Have a good day of teaching!"

How am I going to do this, I'd think. My eyeballs don't even want to move!

But my dear husband, Jim, would deliver me to the university each day where I taught voice. My students would wheel me down the hall for seminars, and sometimes I taught from a reclining lawn chair. I wasn't strong enough to perform as a singer anymore.

Later, Jim would cook me Swiss chard with onions and scrambled eggs, the only food I was able to eat for months.

My oncologist told me my students and my work would get me through it all. And he was right.

Then 35 radiations and big pieces of homemade maple fudge sustained me through the weight loss and weakness. Nothing else tasted good. What else could I do?

Just recently I learned that during that tough breast cancer treatment, doctors had told my husband I probably had only a year to live. His choice not to tell me at the time was wise. He knew that I knew

---

CHAPTER **18:** JEAN THOMAS

how serious that cancer was. And now I know why a minister brought me a book on dying gracefully. I chose to live gracefully!

And in living, my 2nd Act passion was born.

I've always loved to roam the great outdoors. I grew up on a farm, so was always wandering through the woods and along the creeks. Not surprisingly, going through treatment, my world became very small. So I'd read about "far-away places." One of the places I virtually visited was described in Gary Nabhan's book, *The Desert Smells Like Rain*.

The book describes the southern Arizona Tohono O'odham Native American culture and their sacred Baboquivari Peak. The peak is home to the creator, and according to their legend, he resides in a cave below the base of the mountain.

The Tohono O'odham nation considers the peak as the navel of the world: a place where the earth opened and the people emerged after the great flood.

At nearly 8,000 feet tall, that peak became a real spiritual connection for me, too.

After I finished my treatment, I happened to read of a one week Sierra Club service trip near the foot of Baboquivari Peak. I'd have done just about anything to be near that mountain.

So, against my docs' advice for the next three years, I volunteered for that trip.

During the week, we lived in Brown Canyon near the peak on Buenos Aires National Wildlife Refuge. Our job was to remove old barbed wire fence from the grassland section on the refuge.

Crazy for a newly released cancer survivor? Maybe. But I was drawn to be close to that mountain!

When we retired, a year after the last service trip, we were privileged to care for the Education Center on the refuge in Brown Canyon. Our house was a beautiful old adobe, with only emergency radio for communication, and beautiful "Babo" looming protectively over us.

Now that we live in Tucson, my wilderness 2nd Act has grown! The Buenos Aires National Wildlife Refuge is about 70 miles southwest of the city. It's 118,000 acre of "God's Country!" And guess what? I can look out my living room and see my beloved peak!

I've led 135 4-mile guided, interpretive hikes up that pristine mountain canyon. That's 540 miles of climbing – and still counting!

You know, I was in a lovely "box" back in the Midwest: great friends and long hours spent teaching and singing, which I loved. But without those cancers, I would not have found this marvelous new life "out of the box."

CHAPTER **18:** JEAN THOMAS

There was so much for me to learn here in a totally different environment: new cultures, new plants and critters all calling gorgeous Sonoran desert home. I get to share that knowledge and love with everyone who joins me on my hikes.

When I put on my hike-leading uniform, I feel strong! And every time I head down Highway 286 to the refuge, I involuntarily take a deep, relaxing breath, going into my other life.

I invite you to join me. It's a wonderful life!

CHAPTER **18:** JEAN THOMAS

CHAPTER 19

BETHANNE KING-LOBMILLER
Breast Cancer Survivor

BethAnne started Tucson's support group Breastless and Beautiful for women who have chosen not to have reconstruction after mastectomies. It has grown to become an online group with more than 150 members from around the country. Her goal is to educate women of their choice to remain flat and to provide a place of support and understanding for the Breastless and Beautiful. Learn more at *www.facebook. com/breastlessandbeautiful.*

CHAPTER **19:** BETHANNE KING-LOBMILLER

There are women who'll tell you that they've always known that they would get breast cancer. That when they found the lump, they simply knew it was cancer.

I am one of those women. There was always a part of me that knew breast cancer was going to be an up close and personal thing for me.

My grandmother was a cancer survivor. She had her bilateral mastectomy in the mid 1970's. For those who don't know, breast cancer surgery at that time was radical and went deep.

When I was maybe 10 or 11 years old and before I ever un-derstood any of this, I happened upon my grandma changing her blouse in her bedroom. She didn't have any breasts! Her boobies were lying on the bed, inside her bra!

I must have gasped, because when grandma turned and saw the look on my face, she smiled at me and invited me in. She showed me her chest and her scars, although I don't remem-ber her telling me why. She showed me her foobs (fake boobs) and the special bras she wore.

She had different sizes she said, so she could decide how big or small she wanted them to be. In the summer smaller was better because it was cooler.

And sometimes, she said, she didn't wear them at all,

espe-cially when she had her pajamas on. Even now I can't believe I'd never noticed any of this before that day.

There was always a part of me that knew, even before I was diagnosed, that I would not have reconstructive surgery if I lost my breasts.

Although I tell you the decision was already made, accepting the surgery was another thing and another story. Let's suffice it to say that after some time, I have become as comfortable with my body now as I was before the cancer.

Throughout that process, I discovered that there was not much support or advocacy for the flat choice in the breast cancer community.

There are some groups online, but they mostly focus on fash-ion, or breast cancer art, or the politics of insurance. However, there was almost nothing to be found about the choice. The deeper I dug for support on these issues, the more
disappointed I was.

Me? I was lucky. The women who I loved and admired so much, my grandmother, was a role model for me and contin-ues to be in a way she could have never known.

She lived a vibrant life filled with family, love, health and hope. And she did it all without her breasts.

CHAPTER **19: BETHANNE KING-LOBMILLER**

I couldn't bear the pain of women I was meeting who didn't feel good about themselves after their mastectomies. Further, I was compelled to challenge the seemingly widespread and unfair assumption that reconstruction is the wish of ALL wom-en.

So I gave birth to my 2nd Act. I began a group, and became part of the "Flat Movement." In 2015, I founded Breastless and Beautiful, an advocacy and support group for the CHOICE to remain flat after mastectomy.

This amazing group of women supports one another in their choice. They've helped me learn to become comfortable with my body. They've helped me process the changes on how I view myself in the world as a woman without breasts. They've helped me bond with others who have made the same decision, or who are not candidates for reconstruction.

We now have members from around the world. Those who are here in Tucson get together for breakfast and fellowship regularly. Those who aren't local participate in the online community networking. Many women join us before they have surgery. Some find support and are comforted and sometimes relieved to find us and get information. Others discover that reconstruction is the right choice for them. That's what it's all about. Choice – and body love!

This year, we proudly participated in the Tucson Making Strides Against Breast Cancer fundraiser for the American Cancer Society. We need to find the cure for breast cancer, for metastatic breast cancer, for all my pink sisters … and for my daughter and granddaughters too.

Recently my 5-year-old granddaughter asked me, "Grandma, how come you don't have no boobies?"

I did just as my grandmother had done for me. And, when the time is right, I'll share with her the whole story and the reasons behind the choice I made. Most importantly, I'll teach her the beauty of loving her body.

CHAPTER 20

BEV PAUL
Rectal Cancer Survivor

Bev joyfully relocated to Tucson from San Diego to live closer to her grandchildren. Her life philosophy is to fill it with love, kindness and gratitude. Reflecting her passion for helping children, Bev is a "Wish Granter" with the Make-A-Wish organization, and an avid supporter of The Shyann Kindness Project. She also provides onsite meditation services for individuals and businesses. To learn more contact her at:

bevs.bowls@gmail.com.

CHAPTER **20:** BEV PAUL

Love. Gratitude. Kindness. These three words define my 2nd Act.

On the horrifying morning of April 8, 2010 I underwent emergency surgery for rectal cancer at the Tucson Medical Center.

I will always remember the daily visits from my wonderful surgeon and her ever-inspiring words: "Are you ready for some good news, Bev? We were able to remove all of the cancer. It's all gone!" Followed the next day with, "Are you ready for MORE good news, Bev?

I didn't want to frighten you before surgery about the possibility of a colostomy bag. By the smallest measurement possible we were able to re-plumb your system and you won't need the bag."

Considering the level of pain and fear I was in, I certainly could NEVER have imagined all the "good" things that were on their way into my life down the road. And they're still arriving daily today!

Now seven years later I am able to stand here and share this all with you without crying – I hope! I am the healthiest I have ever been in my life.

The healing I have experienced has been on every level, not only physically, but also emotionally, mentally and spiritually.

CHAPTER **20:** BEV PAUL

Coming face to face with death transformed my former issues with depression into the most expansive, constant, complete, total and overwhelming gratitude for every single moment of life.

My desire to LIVE became my primary focus. I now believe that is one of the reasons I succeeded in beating the odds and actually being here today – NOW – as the healthy and happy woman I am.

The struggle was definitely real. My recovery was a 2-year experience of incredible pain and suffering, full of many obstacles to overcome.

I think it's a blessing that we don't know the future. If I had known how hard the recovery was going to be, I may have given up. And if I had given up, I wouldn't be able to now help others on their 2nd Act journeys.

And I wouldn't be here to share the story of my 2nd Act.

Love. Gratitude. Kindness.

The LOVE: In 2014, I became a volunteer with the Make-A-Wish foundation. I am an official Wish Grantor! I get to love children with life threatening illnesses and make their greatest wish come true.

One of my favorite experiences was with a 15 year old boy who had a neurological disorder. He was going blind and his disease could shorten his life.
This young man had two wishes. He was a huge racing

fan and dearly wanted to attend a Nascar event. But he and his family – his parents and four brothers and sisters – had never been out of Tucson.

He'd heard about the fun of a road trip. But because of his illness, there was just never enough money for vehicles or vacations.

And of course what's a road trip without a destination! He put aside his Nascar dream for a road trip to Disneyland with his family.

Now Make-A-Wish always flies people to their destination, but in this case, the family piled into a rented van. They crossed mountains. They walked on the beach. And they whooped it up at Disney.

But I have a friend at Tucson Speedway. A few weeks before his Disney trip, this young man also got a magical night at the racetrack. He met drivers, he rode in a race car around the track, and he even waved the flag at the final race. He touched everyone's heart!

The GRATITUDE: Despite knowing all of the health risks, I was a 35-year smoker. For the last 20 years of that, I had repeatedly tried to quit. In the winter of 2008, I had a horrific case of bronchitis. But I wrapped myself up in a blanket, and coughing and wheezing, went outside for a cigarette. That was my "a ha" moment.

A feeling washed over me totally different from all the other times. And I stopped cold turkey.

CHAPTER **20:** BEV PAUL

I decided to videotape a documentary to duplicate what I was doing daily in an effort to help others. And the HOPE of doing it for others greatly contributed to my own success in finally becoming a non-smoker!

I was so grateful for the life-saving experience, I wrote a book called Your Final Cigarette. In it I outline how to overcome the emotional addiction to nicotine, which is much stronger than the physical addiction.

And I created a six-week program beginning with 14 daily lessons of preparation leading to successfully becoming a non-smoker.

It began as a group workshop, and then broke into one-on-one sessions with people to discover the deep seated emotional reasons for their addiction. My success rate is over 80 percent and the program was even offered at the Cancer Center.

The KINDNESS: I am a volunteer with the Shyann Kindness Project in Tucson.

In 2006 after my friend Sandy and her husband lost their precious daughter Shyann, they circulated cards asking that random acts of kindness be done in Shyann's name. That tiny idea took root and blossomed.

Together with other volunteers we serve low-income schools with a free educational program about kindness. We bring beautiful gifts to the children at each of the schools we visit. And we participate in gift programs during the Thanksgiving and Christmas holiday seasons throughout the Tucson school districts.

To date, the Shyann Kindness Project has touched more than 22,000 Tucson school children. All of our services are 100 percent volunteer and free of charge.

I could go on for much longer, but here's what I hope you'll take home with you today. Life is an awesome gift. We all have endless opportunities to enjoy it, and do whatever we choose to make this place better for ourselves and countless others.

We can all take what we learn from our life challenges and turn them into amazing 2nd Acts. For me, it's love, gratitude and kindness. But there are a million opportunities for you to discover in your 2nd Acts. Follow your heart!

I treasure whatever time I have left on this earth. I am so grateful for all the people who have helped me on this journey of life, as well as THRIVING through cancer.

It is now my total joy to be available, to be the one who can give back in my 2nd Act, and to help others discover theirs.

Love. Gratitude. Kindness.

CHAPTER **20: BEV PAUL**

CHAPTER **21**

LIZ ALMLI
Breast Cancer Survivor

Liz is a physician and breast cancer survivor. She is passionate about her 2nd act: educating, encouraging, and empowering others dealing with the challenges of a cancer diagnosis. She serves as the president of the Tucson Cancer Conquerors and actively raises cancer research funds for the American Cancer Society. Learn more at *www.YouCanConquer.org*.

CHAPTER **21:** LIZ ALMLI

I am a busy wife and mom with a crazy doctor schedule. I did not have time for a breast lump. In October of 2005 after a clear mammogram several months earlier, I found a lump. An ultrasound showed it to be a cyst and they told me to follow-up in six months. I decided to have the cyst removed and just be done with it.

Or so I thought.

The two scariest days in a cancer patient's life: first the call.

"I'm sorry Liz. You have an aggressive, invasive cancer and I did not get it all."

One minute I am feeling strong, healthy, and in control. The next, I am nauseous, weak, and overwhelmed with anxiety. While nothing physically had changed from seconds earlier, my mind was making me physically ill.

Cancer patients are all too familiar with the term "mind race." It's this anxiety provoking experience where your thoughts rapid fire out of your control.

What if my cancer has spread? What if I need chemo, radiation, mastectomies? Will I live to see my children graduate from high school, college, get married? Will I be here for Christmas?

I trained in a trauma center. I learned to stay calm and in control of chaotic situations by preparing for every worst-case scenario that might come crashing through the ER doors.

Blindsided, I was completely unprepared for this crash.

But I was blessed and lucky. Blessed to have an amazing support system of family, friends, and skilled doctors.

And lucky, because a new drug in clinical trials had just been approved by the FDA for my type of cancer.

After a year of chemotherapy, bilateral mastectomies and breast reconstruction, I was ready to put this whole cancer mess behind me.

And then it came: the second scariest day in a cancer patient's life.

Congratulations, you're done! The nurses cheer and give out balloons and hugs. My family says I'm done, my work says I'm done, my doctors say I'm done.

I got into my car and sat in the silence for a moment. Done? My body does not look, or feel, done.

As I drove away from what had been my safety net for the last 12 months, my sense of relief turned into dread. "What if it comes back?"
In every ache and pain lies the imagined total body invasion of a metastatic cancer recurrence. Is this my new normal? My next appointment isn't for three months. A lot can happen in three months! Who is going to take care of me?

CHAPTER **21**: LIZ ALMLI

I was going to have to take care of myself.

It was time for my 2nd Act.

What did I learn from my cancer experience that could help me turn this craziness of survivorship into something positive and productive, empowering myself and others to regain control and stay healthy?

Enter the Tucson Cancer Conquerors!

I passionately serve as the president of this all-volunteer, non-profit organization run by cancer survivors and the people who love them. We understand the physical and emotional challenges that come with a cancer diagnosis and focus on the well-being of the whole person through exercise, nutrition, education, friendship and peer support.

Whether people are newly diagnosed and need someone to sit with them through their first chemotherapy, or just need help moving forward after treatment, we're there. We've been in those shoes. We know what a bad hair day really is!

Our message is "You are not alone."
As Tucson Cancer Conqueror peer supporters, we are positive and encouraging. It's ok to mourn your diagnosis and the loss that it brings, but you cannot get stuck there.

At some point you need to put the tissue box away, surround yourself with people who inspire and support you, and begin to look forward.

Instead of replaying the difficulties of yesterday and worrying about the challenges of tomorrow, it's time to focus on appreciating the gift that is today. None of us knows what tomorrow brings and we certainly don't want to waste even one minute of it!

In this, my 2nd Act, I wanted to share all my lessons with as many survivors as possible.

Lesson 1: I had learned we all need a supporting cast.

Not everyone has someone they can call when they feel overwhelmed, afraid, or discouraged. There had to be something that I, and others who have been through this experience, could do to help.

Lesson 2: I had learned that we need to be mindful of the moments that make us laugh and give us joy.

One morning just after treatment, I was getting ready for work, patiently trying to pencil on a set of matching eyebrows. I am a symmetry nut so this was an ongoing source of my daily frustration.
My husband Scott offered to help, assuring me he could save me lots of time every morning. He then produced a Sharpie and a big smile. While I declined his offer, I was so thankful for his humor.

Lesson 3: I learned that there is something each of us can do.

CHAPTER **21:** LIZ ALMLI

There is an abundance of research in the cancer literature supporting exercise as a way to be stronger during treatment, and as a way to stay healthy.

I became a Certified Personal Trainer with advanced certification as a Cancer Exercise Specialist.

Our Tucson Cancer Conqueror "Get Active" program offers two fitness classes a week, a walking group, a hiking group, and a group of Mindful Meanderers. Our goal is to get survivors active, one baby step at a time.

Recognizing the powerful health benefits of good nutrition, the Tucson Cancer Conquerors also has our very own organic garden. Our members tend and harvest fresh healthy produce with the help of a chef, creating delicious dishes for our monthly birthday dinners. Everyone knows how smart it is to invite a chef to potluck!

Lesson 4: I learned that above all else, we need to find a cure.

I am convinced that I am here today, 12 years later, because of cutting edge research creating new drug therapies. My husband and I became cancer advocates, chairing benefit events and actively fundraising for the American Cancer Society.

If you or your families are dealing with the challenges of a cancer diagnosis, be hopeful. New treatments are in the pipeline every day and we are getting so close. Tomorrow may be the day they find a cure ...YOUR cure. Your job is to keep yourself healthy and strong, physically and emotionally.

Our mission at the Cancer Conquerors is to help. Cancer sucks, but we make it suck less.

I want to leave you all with a powerful quote from Viktor Frankl, an Austrian neurologist, psychiatrist, and holocaust concentration camp survivor.

"Between stimulus and response there is a space. In that space is our power to choose our response. In our response lies our growth and our freedom."

CHAPTER **21:** LIZ ALMLI

CHAPTER **22**

EBONY DANIELS
Breast Cancer Survivor

Ebony has two daughters, Bre and Joy, and a super supportive husband, Jeremy. She is a financial educator, helping families learn financial literacy. She also volunteers teaching youth the importance of saving early. Her video blog, "Fighter to Phoenix," gives women an up close and personal view of the breast cancer journey. Learn more at *www.facebook. com/fightertophoenix/*

CHAPTER **22:** EBONY DANIELS

Take a metaphorical journey with me. I want you to imagine yourself snow skiing, flying down the slopes as fast as you can. You're enjoying the scenery and all that nature has to offer you.

You're not paying attention and then, BAM! You hit a huge rock!

You go flying in the air 100 miles an hour. You hit the ground, and start rolling. You finally stop when you hit a tree. Next thing you know you feel and hear a loud roar. It's an avalanche coming your way but you can't move.

This is EXACTLY how the story of my breast cancer began.

I knew something was wrong when I saw a pea-sized lump in my breast. In your mind, you always hope for the best. But for me, it was not to be.

August 29, 2016 my life changed forever when I heard the dreaded three words NO ONE wants to hear: "You have cancer."

I was in disbelief. After all, my girlfriend had the same lump in her breast. They told her it was a cyst. Surely I had the same outcome. But that was not to be either.

I remember going into a full-blown panic attack and running out of the room with my husband dead on my tail. I threw my hands up and said "Just give me some time, this is a lot for me to process." The nurse and doctor peeked from behind him to ensure I was OK.

When I regained my composure, I went back into the exam room.

They told me that at that time my cancer's stage was unknown. But we all knew my life would never be the same.

As I sat in the car after the diagnosis, my life flashed before my eyes, unanswered questions lingering in my head. Then the sun shined on my face, and I promised myself one thing in silence: I was going to FIGHT!

And so the fight began. It wasn't easy. Things I loved most were being taken away from me by force: time with my family; sitting kneecap to kneecap with families, helping them get out of debt. I am a financial educator; I teach financial literacy. And I volunteer with our youth, teaching them importance of saving early. I missed doing the work I love with people who need me.

I found it very difficult to accept help from my family and friends. When you're used to running the show, it's so hard to let anyone else take the helm.

And I watched my body change before my very eyes. But I am a woman of faith. It was my turn to follow the scripture I had shared often with others: "Be still and

---

CHAPTER **22: EBONY DANIELS**

know that I am God."

I listened, and I knew in my heart that one day everything would return back to me.

Now, I've always been a person who has been very open about my life. I decided if I had to go through this "journey," as I called it, I wasn't going to do it alone. I began making LIVE videos on facebook and reaching out to everyone. Just like that, From Fighter to Phoenix was born and so was my 2nd Act.

Through my From Fighter to Phoenix facebook videos, I hoped that my journey might help other women facing breast cancer. I wanted to show them that it was okay to be scared, to ask for help, to laugh, and to cry. Most of all, I wanted them to know there was light at the end of the tunnel, that they would become someone new, and hopefully someone even stronger, just like the Phoenix rising from the ashes.

To my surprise I received tremendous support. It came in the form of cards and care packages from all over the world. Women were watching and listening!

Now, over a year later, I have become mentally stronger than I ever was! I'm back to doing what I love: spending quality time with my family and helping those around me to do the same.

So, remember my metaphor? This is our lives people. We start out enjoying our lives, working our chosen passions and then we hit a hard place. Sometimes we get knocked from one rock to another. And then we start that downhill spiral.

For me breast cancer was the rock. Flying through the air was what I was missing because everything was moving so fast.

When I rolled down the hill, it represented the fact that my life was about to take a tumble. When I hit the tree, it stunned me, but it also gave me a moment to think about how I got there. And then the avalanche covered me. I could no longer run but had to face everything head on.

In life, you HAVE to remove the unnecessary. You have to plan and reflect on the past so you will not repeat it. But there's one more image in my metaphor. The sun came out and melted the snow away from me.

That represents refreshing your passions and adding new elements to your life because it is what keeps us ALIVE. It's about creating YOUR 2nd Act.

It's about how, no matter what you're challenge, any one of us can go from Fighter to Phoenix!

CHAPTER **22:** EBONY DANIELS

CHAPTER 23

KAY PRINCE
Breast Cancer Survivor

Kay is a seasoned life and success coach, and an authority on how lessons of survivorship can bring joy, passion and purpose to the lives of survivors. As the founder of Emergence, she created self-discovery retreats designed especially for breast cancer survivors. Kay lives in Tucson and volunteers for the Make-A-Wish Foundation. Learn more at *www. emergencementor.com*

It was a beautiful spring day in Denver the kind we dream of all winter long. Our very first grandchild had just been born. And my husband and I were planning dinner with a group of close friends at our favorite Italian restaurant that evening.

I put the top down on my convertible and merrily drove to my chiropractor's appointment, feeling very blessed and grateful for my life. As I sat in the office waiting for my appointment, my cell phone rang and EVERYTHING in my life shifted.

A voice said: "This is Dr. Lucas. Your test results are back and you have breast cancer. We recommend a double mastectomy. Then chemotherapy."

The world stood still.

I walked out of the office, got in my car and drove home to tell my husband. I will never forget the look of terror on his face. He was so afraid — and so was I.

In the following weeks there were appointments, research, and tough decisions to be made. Shortly after my surgery, my husband suggested that a walk would be good.

We went outside and had walked just a few feet down the sidewalk when my husband stopped and turned to me.

"Honey, something's wrong. I feel like I can't breathe.

We've gotta go home."

Within 48 hours I was back in a hospital – this time as an anxious loved one in in the waiting room. My husband had suffered what's called a silent heart attack and was having quadruple bypass surgery.

In just a few short weeks my world had been rocked again to the core. I made some decisions that day as I sat waiting for news about my husband's surgery.

I vowed that I would live every day to the fullest. I committed to deeply loving and cherishing my family and friends, and to focus on creating joy and connection in my life.

As a result of my cancer and his heart attack, my husband and I made some life changing decisions that spring. And my 2nd Act began.

First, I was in charge of all national human resources and recruiting for a rapidly growing financial services company. I'll never forget the day I walked in to the president's office.

"Gerry, I've decided to leave the company."

"You can't leave! This company is so successful and growing like crazy! You'll be getting lots of big bonuses this coming year. You are the engine that helps us grow! You can't go!"
I shared with him my dream to start my own coaching practice. I knew for sure that I couldn't wait. I had

to pursue my passion. He reluctantly accepted my resignation. It was a risky decision, but it was the first step in my 2nd act.

Secondly, our daughter and her husband had another daughter and the family had moved from Denver to Tucson the year before.

As my husband and I continued to examine what was important, we realized that being near them was truly our heart's desire. So we relocated to Tucson. And what a wonderful decision that was!

We so enjoyed our two granddaughters in Tucson, and within a year it got even better: our daughter had twins, a boy, Max, and a girl, Maci. I was blessed to be in the delivery room the day they were born. What a gift!

I continued to expand my coaching business nationally, creating and offering retreats for people experiencing tough life and career transitions like changing careers or going through divorces.

My work always included a focus on living with passion and purpose, and realizing that each of us has special gifts and talents to express.

I was blessed with over 20 years being cancer free, and 20 years of amazing clients who made successful life and career transitions. I felt I was truly making an impact on the lives of others and was very passionate about my work.

CHAPTER **23: KAY PRINCE**

Then one day, sitting at my desk, another unexpected call came in that changed my life. It was from was a client named Diane who had done a retreat with me six years earlier.

She said, "I was diagnosed with intermediate stage breast cancer a year ago. I've just finished a tough year of surgeries and treatment. My breast cancer experience has been life changing.

But since my treatment ended, I feel unsettled about the future. I'm at a loss for what's next in my life. All I know is that I want more meaning and purpose."

She'd talked to many doctors, other survivors, therapists, coaches and had done much research. She could find no one who can help her get her life back on track.

Then she surprised me saying, "I'm calling to ask you if you would consider refining your retreat program for breast cancer survivors."

Wow! Without hesitation I said a hearty yes, yes, yes!

So now my 2nd Act is even bigger with my Emergence Survivorship Program. We offer a weekend retreat called "Creating a Life of Passion, Purpose and Promise," held in Arizona at a guest ranch and in Colorado at a mountain lodge.

You see, if you're a cancer survivor, you know that cancer is truly a life changing experience.

CHAPTER 23: KAY PRINCE

It's leaves us questioning who we are and what we want out of life. Our retreats are a personal formula for what's next, where survivors reconnect with their most joyful times and what matters most. We uncover life meaning and purpose, roast marshmallows at the fire pit, discuss common fears and challenges and hopes and dreams, take nature walks and share yummy meals.

I've been blessed to witness true transformations at our retreats. On the first day of her retreat, a survivor named Jackie saying: "I'm not leading the life I want. I want to get back to who I am."

During the retreat she realized that she was much too focused on her career than her family, often working late. She was ignoring her passions for travel and gardening. She decided that simplifying her life was her goal and at the retreat, created an action plan to do just that.

The last time I spoke with her it was a few minutes after 5 o'clock in the afternoon. This former workaholic was sitting outside with a cup of tea, gazing at her garden. As a result of the retreat, she and her husband had decided to move out of the city into a remote area and downsize. She even bought baby chicks in anticipation of her new country life!
In addition, she and her family were about to leave on a trip to Ireland.

I am so honored and blessed to be working with courageous survivors to re-discover who they are at their very best and to reconnect them with joy and inspiration in their lives.

I look back over the last 20 years. My husband and I thought our lives were blessed before. But our health crises caused us to make changes that are REAL blessings. They are our 2nd Acts. And now my heart sings more than ever!

CHAPTER **23:** **KAY PRINCE**

CHAPTER **24**

TERIE TUTT
Breast Cancer Survivor

Terie is a breast cancer warrior with more than 10 years of survivorship. She is a public relations rep for Radiology Ltd., serves on the Board of Directors for World Care and is a pop-rock professional vocalist. Previously a Development/Volunteer Manager for American Cancer Society, Terie cherishes her family, fur-babies and friends.

CHAPTER **24:** **TERIE TUTT**

I'm one of a blended family of 10 children. We're Italian, Irish, English and Scottish. Consequently we like to dance, sing, eat and, oh boy … don't get us mad!

My strong, amazing, tenacious Mom was a ballroom dance instructor, and my Dad is a professional musician who when I was young did studio session drumming in Dallas and Nashville. In 1969, he had the opportunity to audition for Elvis Presley and got the gig! Whew – it was exactly what he needed to support all of us kids!

At the age of five, I started singing jingles in the Dallas studio. A few of us kids have that music gene. We play instruments or sing and perform today. And if I can boast a second, my 79-year-old Dad is currently the drummer for Neil Diamond. I'm very proud of him.

In 2006, I was 43 and a self-employed entertainer. No, not THAT kind of Entertainer! My band performed for weddings, corporate events, clubs, bar-mitzvahs, you get the idea.

In October of that year during my annual breast exam the doctor found a lump. My head was spinning with the news.

My sister, Christine, only 11 months older than me, we're "Irish Twins," had been diagnosed with breast cancer nine years earlier. I knew what October, Breast Cancer Awareness month was all about. Could it be that I would hear those words that no woman EVER wants to hear? I couldn't and wouldn't say them until it was confirmed.

A mammogram was ordered which revealed "suspicious findings." It was followed by all the diagnostic tools needed to confirm those "suspicious findings."
After a sleepless night, my doctor called to say those dreaded words: "I'm sorry, you have breast cancer."

I lost it for a bit, and then picked myself up off the floor.

I looked in the mirror and said "Cancer, you picked the wrong girl to mess with!" I was, after all, Italian, Irish, English and Scottish.

I wanted that cancer out of my body to begin the new year cancer free. So we scheduled my lumpectomy for late December.

At the same time my Aunt Dot was diagnosed with aggressive brain cancer. We knew she didn't have much time. I contemplated whether to tell her about my breast cancer.

After talking with my Uncle Felix (who himself had lung cancer), we knew that she would be so mad if she found out and I hadn't told her. So I did. I was glad we could share that experience before she passed later that month.

CHAPTER 24: TERIE TUTT

On surgery day, the doctor asked, "If we remove your centennial node and find that cancer is in your lymph nodes, do you want me to do a mastectomy?"

My response: "You bet, give me new perky ones!" Thank goodness it was not in my lymph nodes! They're perky anyway!

Chemo was up next. I was terrified on my first day, but when I arrived I heard laughing. There were other warriors in there!

When I moved on to radiation, Karen was there from my support group and on the same radiation schedule! We held "board/survivor meetings," giggling and talking until each of us was called back.

At our support group, we exercised, shared stories and supported each other. And that's where my 2nd Act began. You see, even though we were all dealing with cancer, we kept positive attitudes.

Cancer might have been taking a toll on our bodies, but it was not going to take our spirit.

Meanwhile, back on the singing front, I tried wigs over my bald head, but they were just too hot under the stage lights. And that experience debuted another facet of my 2nd Act.

I decided to be bald and beautiful while performing. My attitude was that hair and breasts didn't define me as a woman or an entertainer. And I wanted to evoke conversation, hopefully to support others I met. And it did.

People would ask, why are you bald? I would share my story and many times ended up crying with someone who had been through cancer or who had a survivor family member.

Next, I began fundraising for Making Strides Against Breast Cancer and later took a position with the American Cancer Society. I wanted to give back and make this scary journey easier for anyone else.

I worked long, hard, emotional hours. But my reward was meeting extraordinary survivors, caregivers and their families.

And then cancer touched my family again. I lost my brother, aunt, uncle and cousin. My sister, unfortunately, was re-diagnosed after 10 years of survivorship. But I'm so thankful she survived the beast a second time.

My 2nd Act journey finally took me to the amazing job I have today as a Professional Relations Representative for Radiology Limited.

Because of our community outreach program called RadCommunity, I'm here today to give back again. Last year, Judy reached out to us and our partnership began. I truly believe that God puts in one another's paths for a reason.

CHAPTER 24: TERIE TUTT

So what truths have I learned on this long and winding 2nd Act journey? There's no better time to be happy than right now. If not now, when? Our lives will always be filled with challenges.

So I say to you today, Don't wait to live your best life, until you lose 10 pounds, gain 10 pounds after treatment, or until your kids move out. Don't wait until you finish getting your MBA, get married, move or change jobs. Don't wait until you get a new car or your home is paid off.

Don't wait or until winter, spring, summer or fall. All you gotta do is call, and I'll be there, living my 2nd Act!

CHAPTER **25**

MEREDITH MITSTIFER
Ovarian Cancer Survivor

Meredith has been with the the Federal Bureau of Prisons for 10 years as a Licensed Clinical Psychologist. Previously, she was a psychologist for the Arizona Department of Corrections Death Row and Special Management Units. Meredith volunteers on the Board of Directors for the National Ovarian Cancer Coalition which raises awareness, research and improves quality of life for ovarian cancer survivors and their families. Learn more at *www.ovarian.org*.

CHAPTER **25:** MEREDITH MITSTIFER

Ovarian cancer has been referred to as the disease that whispers. Whispers? Why?

Symptoms exist – but can be vague. Vague means late detection. Late detection means less survival rate. Less survival rate means less survivors. Less survivors means less awareness. Less awareness means more affected. More affected means more silence. More silence means whispers go unheard.

FEEL THE TEAL?

Ovarian cancer, although rare – is deadly. 22,000 diagnosed,14,000 will die. Do the math – it's over half.

FEEL THE TEAL?

There is no test. There is no cure. Variations are too many. Lives are changed. Futures affected. Relationships challenged. Mothers lost. Spouses pass. Parents feel helpless. Child bearing hopes removed. 2nd Acts … stolen.

FEEL THE TEAL?

Why Teal? Teal is the color of Ovarian Cancer Awareness. The world needs to feel the teal, in order to stop the whisper.

This is my tribe. My teal tribe. My teal tribe is fighting. My teal tribe is dying. My hope, drive and 2nd Act?

CHAPTER **25:** MEREDITH MITSTIFER

For ALL to FEEL THE TEAL

Beginning at age 19 I struggled with gynecological issues.

Pain, discomfort, multiple surgeries, all with limited results. Next came infertility issues.

The isolation, feelings of brokenness ... indescribable. I began to seek alternative options, tests and procedures. Insemination finally scheduled. Then canceled. An unknown mass found? More waiting. More wondering. Consultations occurred. Five percent chance of cancer. I opted to wait and see if the unknown mass ... just became unknown.

FEEL THE TEAL?

Mass tripled in size. Surgery scheduled immediately. Pre-operative tests mandate a pregnancy test. Really?

Not fair. Pour gas on my fire. So I pee in the cup. Let's get this over with.

Wait. Results in. Brakes slammed. Nurses in tears. I'm pregnant? Naturally? Options are changed. Abort and proceed with surgery. Or wait four months. I exit.

FEEL THE TEAL?

Fifteen years ago, I was 30 years old, had surgery when I was four months pregnant, and was diagnosed with ovarian cancer. The fetus survived. Time stood still. Darkness tried to steal my soul. Life and death inside me, at the same time. Second opinions, future surgeries, waiting on treatment.

Questioning the lack of research, questioning the course of action, questioning myself and the life of my child.

FEEL THE TEAL?

Indecisiveness everywhere, vulnerabilities exposed. Seeing the fear in my parents' eyes – words cannot capture. Looking at my womb. Fearing the future for my legacy. Breathe. Kick forward. It was prenatal care – but with a twist.

FEEL THE TEAL?

Baby arrives five weeks early. Lung deficits. Requires neonatal care for a month. Chemo begins in six weeks. Independence stripped, hair falling out, husband informs me he didn't really mean in sickness and in health.

Move across country, parents assume care of me and my newborn. Humbled. Scared. Alone. Grateful for their love and toxic free space. The plot twists of my first act – never forgotten – shaped me for my 2nd Act.

FEEL THE TEAL?

2nd Act – relinquished control. Realized I could not and will not do this alone. Rode the waves the best I could. Finished treatment. Returned home. Completed doctorate.

Got divorced. Little did my ex-husband know how he motivated me to change my research and dissertation to focusing on perceived partner adaptations to a cancer diagnosis. PAUSE Chapter closed.

FEEL THE TEAL?

The 2nd Act was of existing, being, and living fearlessly authentic. Stop running. Start embracing. Making every day count and fulfill my mission – to inspire Tucson to Feel the Teal.

I began to attend events sponsored by an organization called the National Ovarian Cancer Coalition while I was in treatment. I later joined as a volunteer and then for a few years, managed the local Tucson chapter. I did not want anyone to walk this journey alone. This role, this 2nd Act, allowed me to connect to other Ovarian Survivors and their families.

Quality of life programs and events in a world – not very TEAL AWARE – provided a circle of support. A tribe. A sense of belonging, despite hating the membership criteria.

Here is where I learned advocating for myself. And it allowed me to naturally advocate for others. I began

---

CHAPTER **25:** MEREDITH MITSTIFER

public speaking and attending events, sharing my story, my vulnerabilities. I was featured in a video called "Scarred Beautiful," exposing not only the physical scars of this disease, but the mental and emotional.

I began to use my voice as a catalyst for connection, support and advocacy of our TEAL TRIBE.

I began to speak my truth.

We all have a story. We need each other, and others need us. Too many women are facing this battle alone.

Vulnerable … lost … fearful and unaware. Bearing witness to their stories hopefully empowers them to embrace their own 2nd Act.

FEEL THE TEAL?

In 2015, I was asked to join the NOCC board of directors on a more national level. New mission: inspire the world to feel the TEAL. Excited. Overjoyed.

I was provided a platform to share my story, support research, increase local community events in multiple states, and be part of creating and providing programs that improve the quality of life for ovarian cancer survivors, their loved ones, caregivers and families.

FEEL THE TEAL?

Should the battle be lost, the tribe is never forgotten.

CHAPTER **25:** MEREDITH MITSTIFER

Don't get me wrong – it's heart wrenching. I have witnessed firsthand people in pain and I have watched my friends die. However, I refuse to let their battles go unnoticed, or their loved ones suffer alone.

I will use my voice for others that have been silenced by this horrible disease. I can truly say, I LOVE this 2nd Act! I hope to inspire others to find their 2nd Acts, their voice, speak their truth and find their circle, their tribe.

I want to ensure a legacy of advocacy and support that continues long after I expire. My son, my legacy, has been advocating since birth. He is the momentum of this entire 2nd Act. He simply sets my life to song. My feet are grounded, my heart is open and I am profoundly honored to share sacred space, support, tears, laughter, inspiration and love with my teal tribe in this 2nd Act of Life.

No more whispers. No more silence.
FEEL THE TEAL!

CHAPTER **25: MEREDITH MITSTIFER**

PHOENIX

When we think of stage shows, we think of bright lights and stars. And this performance was no different as it introduced the new name of our performances:

It featured eight amazing bright lights in the form of eight amazing survivor stars.

There was one more bright light this performance brought to mind. Elana Wight, part of our 2017 Phoenix cast, became a heavenly star on January 27, less than a year after her 2nd Act performance. While her death broke our hearts, we celebrate the woman she was: one of humor, grace and courage.

Sunday, March 18, 2018 3:00 p.m
Peoria Center for the Performing Arts, Peoria, AZ

This performance was made possible by the generosity of SMIL, Sir Speedy – Glendale, and Front Doors Magazine

Love to Olivia Fierro, Emcee
AZ Family's 3 TV

CHAPTER **26**

ANDREA BORG
Acute Myeloid Leukemia Survivor

Andrea is a wife, mother and former corporate executive. After beating leukemia, she wrote *The Mindset Cure: How I Beat My 90 Day Death Sentence*, and speaks about her journey to health and the lessons she learned. She has lead a Girl Scout troop for 25 years, and is on the Girl Scout Council board. Learn more about her at *AndreaBorg.com*.

I'd like to invite you to take a journey with me.

Six years ago, I was a corporate executive, wife, mother and serial volunteer. That July, I got the report from my annual physical – my health was perfect! But four months later, my hands hurt and I couldn't close them.

The doctor said I had a virus and prescribed steroids and antibiotics. I felt better for a few days, but the pain returned. More steroids, more antibiotics, again brief relief.

After five months of various diagnoses, I had an appointment at Mayo Clinic. Finally, I thought, I'll have an answer to what is ravaging my body. Now I can take a pill and get back to my life.

The doctor – stoic – and I – hopeful – square off over his desk. He spoke. "You have less than 90 days to live.

"You have a very aggressive form of Acute Myeloid Leukemia. We can try to treat you, but we don't know if we'll be able to help you. Or we can send you to hospice."

My world stopped. I heard only two things, "90 days to live" and "hospice." I was plunged into darkness. Fear gripped my throat, making breathing difficult. I fell into despair. I felt powerless.

That was my pivotal moment. I had to make a choice. I could choose to be a victim; I could fall into "Oh my

God! I'm going to die!" panic. Or I could choose to be an active participant in my return to health. I could set aside my fear, my powerlessness, my despair. The question I faced was, do I live in hope? Or die in pain?

I chose life.

After four rounds of chemo, a bone marrow transplant and a long recovery, I was questioning. Questioning why I had lived. Questioning what I was to learn and what was next for me.

The answer to "why did I live" was simple and clear: to be of service. I was to examine my difficult path and unearth gold that could be spent in helping others.

The answer to what I was to learn was more perplexing. After months of introspection, I realized there were two lessons.

First was understanding of why I got sick. The second was grasping how I beat my death sentence. The doctors determined there was no hereditary or environmental reason I had gotten leukemia. After much research and reflection, it came to me: I was to blame for my disease.

I'd allowed it to ravage my body by being an "always-on," multitasking perfectionist super woman. I created unsustainable levels of stress and crippled my immune system.

The nugget of gold in this discovery was that I needed

CHAPTER **26:** ANDREA BORG

to become a recovering perfectionist if I was to remain healthy.

When considering why I beat the odds, I read stories from other survivors and scoured books that discussed the power of the mind in overcoming seemingly insurmountable physical and emotional challenges.

I began to understand the power that my unshakable vision of surviving the disease had played in my recovery. That vision had shut out the fear, despair and powerlessness that threatened to overtake me.

I chose not to be a victim of the disease. This gold nugget was possibly even more powerful than the first nugget I had uncovered.

With these discoveries, my excitement grew. I knew my lifestyle had allowed my disease to take root. I saw people around me following the same destructive path. I understood the risks they couldn't see.

Cha-ching!

I had a little gold. I could help them!

I knew my mindset had been key to my survival. As I talked to people, I realized that everyone I knew had been touched by cancer — either as a patient or as the loved one of someone who had suffered with the disease.

Many of those who walked the cancer path had the same powerful mindset I had to propel them through. Others let dark fear overtake them. I had walked through the same fear, I understood their pain. It was hard to maintain the survival mindset.

Cha-ching!

Gold was raining down because I knew I could help them!

Helping was my mission! But how? Talking to people at meetings, parties and events, having conversations on airplanes, trains and busses was great. I loved those conversations.

I felt I was bringing hope and inspiration to those I spoke with. But how many people could I realistically help one-on-one? The answer was "not nearly enough."

In my quest to reach a larger audience, I began to write blogs about my experience. But I soon realized that my platform wasn't big enough.

I contemplated how to reach not just hundreds, but thousands and even millions of people who needed to hear my message. The vision of a book emerged. And that vision ultimately resulted in the release of my first book last October called *The Mindset Cure: How I Beat My 90-Day Death Sentence.*

And that vision has produced the outline for my second book called *Better Than Yesterday: Strategies for*

CHAPTER **26:** ANDREA BORG

Shifting Your Mindset to Win at Life. It will be released in 2018.

I've received wonderful feedback from people who read my first book. They said that it had helped them through tough times. Some even declared, "Your book changed my life!"

The thought of changing lives drives me.

There are many ways to reach people. For many, books are the avenue, but for even more, the personal touch is more powerful. They want to see the person and hear their voice.

I know I need to speak. Speak wherever people are gathered and willing to listen. This is my inaugural speech to a large group; YOU are my first big audience!

I've also been invited to audition for a TEDx Talk about how I used my power mindset to beat my death sentence.

I know the broad reach of TEDx will allow me to touch large audiences and bring my message to those who need to hear that they are not powerless. They can choose to not let fear and despair overcome them even in the face of one of the most dreaded diseases. My mission is clear: to change the world, one cancer diagnosis at a time.

CHAPTER **26:** ANDREA BORG

CHAPTER **27**

PATTY ORTEGA
Uterine, Kidney and Thyroid Cancer Survivor

Patty, the mother of five amazing children and a Valley realtor, believes in building wealth through real estate, mindfulness and compassion. She is a dedicated volunteer with Face In the Mirror, and brings hope and inspiration to Hispanic women cancer survivors. Learn more about her at *FaceIntheMirror.org.*

CHAPTER **27:** PATTY ORTEGA

Standing before you is a channel of love and infinite possibilities. I know that anything is possible, because I am living proof of it.

For me to realize this, all it took was cancer – THREE TIMES: uterine cancer in 2007, kidney cancer in 2009 and thyroid cancer in 2012. And I would endure all of them again if it meant that I get to be as happy as I am today.

Those diagnoses are all vivid moments that have passed, but they served as the most important chapters of my life. I realize now that if I had died, I would have never lived.

Before cancer, I thought of myself as just another statistic: a Hispanic girl from the East L.A. projects, with a failed marriage, five children (all of whom are amazing, by the way), and no true direction. My list of victim roles was ongoing.

I saw success as only available for people outside of my neighborhood. That was the biggest lie I told myself. I now know that success is different for everyone. For me, it varies from day to day, but it always ends with gratitude. Gratitude first for God: He always has me in the right place at the right time, and gives me His blessings, even if I can't see them at that moment.

And I'm grateful for my cancers. Without them, I wouldn't have met so many amazing and courageous women. I wouldn't have discovered how strong I really

CHAPTER **27:** PATTY ORTEGA

am, or had a story to share. It is the story of my 2nd Act.

Sixteen years ago, a wonderful woman named Barbara MacLean began an organization called Face in the Mirror in honor of her sister's cancer journey. Barbara realized that while patients may receive cutting edge medical care in the hospital, the staff simply doesn't have the time to do more than basic personal hygiene.

Face in the Mirror goes those extra steps. Volunteers moisturize women's faces, put on a little makeup, fluff their hair, or give them wigs. And men aren't forgotten either. They receive shaves, hair combing, and hand and foot massages.

And every month Face in the Mirror holds their famous teas. Imagine a room full of women cancer survivors sharing tea, desserts and stories. It was a scene I couldn't have imagined, until my first experience eight years ago. I felt as if I had suddenly been granted permission to love and care for myself.

I soon realized what I got from Face in the Mirror I wasn't supposed to keep. It had been loaned to me to share with those around me. And that's just what I've done!

Sometimes Barbara asks me to say a few words to the ladies gathered at the teas. Other times, I speak with them individually. I tell them there is light at the end of every tunnel. Each of us has the opportunity to become the light for someone else. But to be that light, we first must feel the burn.

And this leads me to the second part of my 2nd Act. Like many survivors, I asked God the infamous question: Why me?

It took time to finally understand that He needs me to stand for those who need self-love, to empower those who have self-doubt, and to guide those who feel lonely to groups like Face in the Mirror. My community desperately needs all of those things. Mothers and daughters, sisters and friends, we Hispanic women put others' health needs before our own, sometimes to our own detriment. And as a whole, we are less aware of available resources.

What I once thought to be a disadvantage – being a Hispanic woman – I now use as a driving force to take information to those ears and hearts that need it. It took me five years to finally see an important lesson in my cancers. God has blessed me with a voice to project and share all that is possible with women who are like me.

I share with them that we all have to face battles. Each of us feels ours must be the most difficult. But if we look at them from a slightly different angle, we'll see the beauty behind it all. There are no accidents, no coincidences. There are hidden blessings in every struggle. Things have always been, and will continue to be, perfect just as they are.

And I tell them that everything, the good and the

atrocities, have shaped me into the PHENOMENAL woman that I am today.

Phenomenal … it has taken almost my entire adult life to believe that this is so. Now I can say it and believe it in my heart. That's probably the BEST part of my 2nd Act!

So here we are in 2018. This year, my goal isn't to reach a sales milestone, to lose weight or anything close to that. My goal is simple: to open my heart even more. It is only then that we receive gratification.

I get that in order for us to love who we are today, we can't hate the experiences that shaped us. In adversity, if we can keep love, respect and hope close, everything is possible.

My wish for you is to walk this earth every day with gratitude, love and an open heart.

CHAPTER 28

ROSE PATTI
Two-time Breast Cancer Survivor

Rose is a native of Ohio, with an MBA in Marketing, and a JD. She is a happily married, happily retired attorney who considers herself an ambassador for all the wonderful cancer resources available to Arizona survivors. She also considers herself a "wiganado," a person who loves wigs!

CHAPTER **28:** ROSE PATTI

You've heard of "A Tale of Two Cities." Well, I'm going to tell you "A Tale of Two Breasts." I am a two-time breast cancer survivor – in 1992 and 2015 – with a basal cell skin cancer thrown in for good measure.

In 1992, I was diagnosed with stage 1 estrogen-positive breast cancer. I had a lumpectomy, chemotherapy and radiation.

The standard of care was not to do chemo with a Stage 1 cancer. But I decided to enter a randomized clinical trial whose results would help women around the world. Lucky me, my name was picked to be one of those receiving chemo.

I had beautiful long hair at the time, and of course it started falling out. I saved it in a shoe box. I'm not sure why. I guess I thought I could glue it back on one day.

At the time, I was a litigation attorney and I worked through my chemo and radiation. I thought to myself, "I'll bet this chemo is going to make me go through menopause. I'm still young – I was 42. Will I get old and wrinkly?"

My oncology nurse had wise words: "The people who looked bad before, look bad afterwards. The people who looked good before, look good afterwards!"

And she was right. I did end up looking like my old self. And when I had completed the treatment, my life

CHAPTER **28:** ROSE PATTI

really took off!

I loved to dance and started dancing again. I became an amateur competitive ballroom and swing dancer. And I got married for the first time to a fabulous man. Overall life was good, except for my breasts.

My radiated breast seemed to be shrinking, while the un-radiated breast seemed to be growing. So my husband and I named the little one "Peanut" and the big one "Hot Dog."

When I moved to Arizona from Ohio, I wanted to have a network of cancer doctors and resources in my hip pocket. Being a researcher, I wanted to learn what was available to me, so I went to a symposium at St. Joseph Hospital and asked questions.

At the break, an audience member approached me. She was able to answer some of my questions and gave me her card.

"I work at Tina's Treasures at the Virginia Piper Cancer Center," she told me. "Come see me some time."

Since I lived close by, I dropped in and shared my challenges with little Peanut and gigantic Hot Dog. She fixed me up a lovely prosthetic for Peanut and a bra to hold them all together.

The prosthetic – a piece of fake boob – made Peanut the same size as Hot Dog. I was golden. I had even boobs!

CHAPTER **28:** ROSE PATTI

But there were more wonderful programs at Virginia Piper: yoga, art classes, nutrition classes and more. I now call that place my "day camp."

As I met people there, I would ask them who their doctors were and what their experiences had been. And I always saved the information.

Then in November, 2015, 24 years after my first diagnosis, I was diagnosed with triple negative breast cancer in my left breast. Yup, poor Hot Dog got cancer (although Peanut was still being good.)

Of course I was in shock. How could I go from estrogen positive breast cancer in Peanut to triple negative years later in Hot Dog? No one had an answer for that.

It was stage 1 again. But there is no targeted therapy for triple negative and it is an aggressive cancer. So again, I was scheduled to have chemo. And again I would add to my shoe hair box.

The three months before I started chemo, I was a zombie. Luckily, I had a supportive husband, and wonderful friends in Arizona and Ohio who called and visited me. They helped, but I was still terrified of the chemo.

But you know what? After the treatments became part of my routine, I realized they were not as scary as I had expected.

And here's the best part. I had a double mastectomy

CHAPTER **28:** **ROSE PATTI**

– a free boob job! No more Peanut and Hot Dog. And they're fabulous! But enough about my boobs.

Let me tell you about the amazing survivorship community I discovered in the Valley of the Sun.

We support one another through some of our darkest days. We can honestly say, "I understand. I've been there." We are a sisterhood of survivors. And because of the 2nd Acts of many, my 2nd Act was born.

You have probably surmised from my shoe box, that my hair was a really big deal to me.

Before I even started chemo the second time, I contacted Don't be a Chump! Check for a Lump! created by Holly Rose, who you'll hear from shortly. They provided me with a free brand new wig which I got to pick out. What a godsend!

And while I was at the wig store I saw a card for Face in the Mirror, which Patty just told you about. I asked the salesperson to tell me more. She said, they also give away wigs. I thought, "I could use a second wig."

I contacted them, and realized a pattern was forming – some may even call it an "addiction." Each time I got a wig, I wanted another. I became a Wig-a-nado.
I can be a blonde … or a brunette … or a redhead … or a silver fox. Baldness was no longer my curse, but a lovely excuse to be anything I wanted to be! Talk about making lemonade out of lemons! And I shared the wacky benefit of being bald with my chemo – and

CHAPTER **28:** ROSE PATTI

hair challenged – sister survivors every chance I got.

Best of all, in getting to know these wonderful, wig-giving organizations, my 2nd Act became more defined.

Suddenly, it hit me like a 2nd Act ton of bricks! There are lots of wonderful cancer resources available. But finding them requires research.

Just seeing a list of their services on a website does not do them justice. That requires conversations. There was no one person to tell you about them. And that required someone like me.

I am the one-on-one resource to tell other patients, along with short and long term survivors, what is available, and it's not just wigs.

It's free skin products, exercise programs, lymphedema treatment, and more. I created a backpack that I cart around with me. It contains dozens and dozens of brochures, flyers, and business cards I've found so I can share them on the spot with patients and survivors as I meet them.

I call it Gratitude in a Backpack! I have GRATITUDE for these resources because they have made my life happier and continue to make it happier through my survivors. So my resources are gratefulness resources.

I started passing out materials when I was doing chemo. I would approach other women patients and tell them about the free wigs or the tea parties or whatever information I had that might cheer them up and make them happy.

At this point, I am happy that my 2nd Act is very grassroots. I'm okay not being a survivorship big wig. I am just a little wig – who happens to love wigs!

Now when I meet someone at the Virginia Piper Center who I can help, I tell them. When I go to the plastic surgeon and I see the women with scared faces, I tell them. No matter where I meet women survivors, I tell them.

And now I'm telling you.

CHAPTER 28: ROSE PATTI

CHAPTER **29**

CHERYL LAFLEN
Breast, Kidney and Lung
Cancer Survivor

Cheryl is a longtime Mesa resident with nearly 40 years as a community activist and volunteer. She is a mother, grandmother, caregiver to her 89-year-old mom, as well as being an author. Cheryl shares openly the good, the bad and the scary sides of the cancer experience, always "blooming where she has been planted!"

CHAPTER **29**: CHERYL LAFLEN

I am so happy to be here. Here, with you, certainly, but also HERE – as in alive, living, breathing and grateful for every wonderful minute of the day!

In 2000, my husband, Milt, and I joined an organization established by Dwight Eisenhower over 60 years ago called Sister Cites. Cities across the U.S. connect with cities around the world to build friendships and a path to peace, one relationship at a time.

They share humanitarian, cultural, economic and exchange programs, all to make the world a better place. It was a vision and mission that captured our hearts.

Along the way, we have met so many wonderful people wherever we go, from the senior center in Mexico, to a medical clinic in Peru, to the orphanages of South Africa, the pyramids of Egypt and the Taj Mahal in India.

I'm telling you this because Sister Cities has played a big part in my healing, and my 2nd Act. And it has allowed me to support friends beyond the borders of Arizona.

I had a wonderful career as a school librarian. I loved my job right up to the day I retired. Nine days later I was diagnosed with breast cancer.

Many members of my medical team had been with us at the clinic in Peru. I knew them. They were friends.

CHAPTER **29**: CHERYL LAFLEN

I was blessed to have them caring for me through this new journey. I never felt fear or anxiety.

I chose to have a bilateral mastectomy, followed by chemotherapy. I have no regrets for making this choice. Indeed, I have the best of all worlds. I can go larger or smaller whenever I choose and if I want, I can even leave "the girls" at home in the drawer.

Now, be honest, aren't there times you wish you could do that? And I certainly believe my golf swing is much better!

By taking one day at a time I regained my strength, and became the queen of pink, an advocate for survival to the newly diagnosed, and their families, one of whom was my sister.

Sister Cities was still a passion for us. And growing that passion has played an important part of my 2nd Act. At one meeting, I was seated at a table with mayors from cities in Israel, Syria and Palestine. How inspiring it was to hear them commit to working together for peace.

Later, I was able to help a Sister Cities friend in Guaymas, Mexico, whose wife was diagnosed with breast cancer.

He told me mastectomy supplies were not as available for them there as they were for me here. When I got home, I sent my new Sister Survivor in Mexico bras and prosthetics so she could feel as good about herself again as I had.

I also went back to school and became a Certified Nursing Assistant to expand my abilities in my volunteer missions. I founded the "September Concert" in Mesa after the 9 -11 attacks. It was an effort to use music to help heal our community and for it, I was given the Spirit of Sister Cities award for that year.

Life was good and there was great relief when I passed the magic "five year" mark.

Then, in 2014, while checking for arthritis, my doctor found a tumor on my kidney. "Almost always malignant," he said. More tests found an attached blood clot that had grown very close to my heart and we had a difficult time finding a doctor to do the operation.

I had my surgery at the U. of A. Medical Center in Tucson. I didn't think I would survive this time, especially since I was a Sun Devil in Wildcat territory! But God had another plan, and I came through the surgery. It was great to be alive.

And when we were asked to expand our Sister Cities responsibilities, Milt and I agreed to lead the organization for the state of Arizona. We hosted exchange students on trips to the Grand Canyon and our mountain cabin. We volunteered in the boutique run by Tempe to fund their many programs. We

CHAPTER 29: CHERYL LAFLEN

221

traveled all over Arizona to grow and establish new programs for peace.

Although I hadn't received any post-surgery treatment for my kidney cancer, I knew there was a strong chance that it might have spread. We weren't surprised, then, when 15 months later, three small spots showed up in my lung.

I had surgery to remove one lobe of my right lung on December 18, 2015, and made it home to share the beauty of Christmas with my family. I had a new scar, but was once again cancer free. My daughter has told a friend her mom is like "swiss cheese." How's that for an image?

Taking it one day at a time, I was soon up to full speed. I had begun writing my memoirs as a hobby, and by this time had a couple of notebooks full of stories.

Milt started pushing me to put them in a book and, with his encouragement, Glimpses was published in time to be the family Christmas gift of 2016.

Sharing our family stories was an important part of my 2nd Act. I wanted everyone to understand that a cancer diagnosis – even three of them – was not the same as a death sentence!

Of course, we were still giving a lot of time to growing and empowering Sister Cities organizations in Arizona. And I was amazed to receive a call from

CHAPTER **29:** **CHERYL LAFLEN**

Roheet, another Sister Cities friend from Agra City, India.

His mother-in-law had been diagnosed with stage IV breast cancer and he wanted to leave no stone unturned in helping her. He asked if I would connect him to my doctor.

My doctor was quick to respond and happy to help. Again, my Sister Cities world and my 2nd Act world crossed paths.

Many people speak of the gifts cancer has given them and, as hard as that might be to believe, it is true. The gift of awareness is a big one. As a survivor, you don't take things for granted anymore. The beauty of a sunset, the kindness of a friend, the joy of family, the support of that special caregiver and the opportunity to make a difference are the things that count.

The 2017 Sister Cities state conference was in the planning stages and Milt and I were always busy. It was the start of Memorial Day Weekend when I took Milt to the emergency room for a minor issue. But the doctor pronounced a diagnosis we weren't prepared for.

"You have cancer in all major organs," he told Milt.
It was melanoma and he lived just 17 days. I can tell you, it is much more difficult to be on the caregiver side of the cancer experience.

So, here I am. Is this my 5th or 6th act? I am not sure.

CHAPTER 29: CHERYL LAFLEN

Day by day, I continue working to make a difference through the Sister Cities Youth Ambassadors program.

My 2nd Act has expanded even more to include volunteering with cancer patients in the East Valley.

I never planned to be in this particular garden. But I am committed to this: I will bloom where I am planted!

CHAPTER **30**

KIMBERLY BRANCHE
Multiple Myeloma

Kimberly is the founder and CEO of Branche Basu Boutique, LLC. She has been Johnny's wife for 23 years and the mother of three. She believes in the 3 F's: faith, family, and friends. She's pursuing a doctoral degree in Marriage and Family Counseling to help families going through personal struggles. Learn more about her at *www.branchebasuboutique.com*.

CHAPTER **30:** **KIMBERLY BRANCHE**

I remember like it was yesterday. I was sitting on the side of the bathtub, my head down. My husband walked into the bathroom and asked, "What are you doing?"

I looked up at him, confused, thinking, are you serious? Didn't we just leave the same place together?

But I'm getting ahead of myself.

As I look back over my life, I have always been a busy bee. (Sings "I've Got a Testimony").

Some call it the ministry of help and services. I call it extreme volunteer syndrome.

I was the Booster Club president, secretary and web designer, the Praise Dance leader, a Bible Study teacher, and a youth leader. You name it, I was it!

I have always been that person who helps when there is a need to be met. My body seemed fine with this until I began to feel burned out, with brain fog and joint pain.

I decided to see my rheumatologist, Dr. Randy. She told me she would get to the bottom of my issues by running every test possible until she found the answer. That would be fine, I told her, as long as my insurance covered it.

Finally I got a call to come in and go over my lab

results. I arrived with notepad and pen.

"Okay Dr. Randy," I said. "What's going on?" (As if I was her PA.)

She went through everything before she finally mumbled the words "Multiple Myeloma." I was numb.

She said, "You're young" – I was 38 – "and that's a good thing."

Dr. Randy referred me to Palo Verde Cancer Specialists, where the oncologist confirmed to my husband and me that I had Multiple Myeloma. It is a blood disease, a cancer of the plasma cells. She, too, assured me that because I was young, I could fight the disease.

Cancer. I had a daughter who had just graduated from high school and was starting her freshman year in college. My son was in his senior year of high school. And my youngest daughter was graduating from 8th grade.

I thought about my dad dying from lung cancer my senior year of high school.

He missed all the events as I grew into adulthood. "Lord please," I said, "don't let this happen to me."

I was scheduled for a bone marrow biopsy and more lab work. The plan was six months of chemotherapy, followed by a stem cell transplant.

CHAPTER **30**: KIMBERLY BRANCHE

Remember my story of sitting on the side of the tub? That was day it happened, right after this visit. As soon as my husband and I got home, I headed straight upstairs and sat on the side of the tub. I was going to have my own pity party and no one was invited.

My husband came in and asked what was wrong with me. "Were you not just with me in the doctor's office? I asked him. "Did you not hear them say I had cancer?"

"But, he said, "did you not hear what else they said? Just wait and see. Don't get ahead of yourself."

I thought about my kids and the unfinished business in my life. I hadn't lived long enough. This couldn't be how it was all going to end.

Weeks went by, then months, and no chemotherapy, delayed by battles with my insurance company.

I was filled with mixed emotions. Should I be grateful I wasn't having chemo? Or should I panic because I still had cancer?

I retreated to the bathroom again. Yep, it's my hiding place. Again, my husband found me there.

"Don't you trust God?" he asked. "You have to believe in what you teach others. Where is your faith?" He reminded me to listen to God's words, to pray and seek Him.

This time, I left that bathroom empowered and ready

CHAPTER **30:** KIMBERLY BRANCHE

to fight back.

I began educating myself about Multiple Myeloma, looking for ways not only to give back, but to LIVE in the process. I wanted to find out where the disease had come from and if I could keep it from becoming even more serious. And I began changing everything.

I removed toxic relationships and bad food habits. I stopped drinking Coke – my go-to drink – and stopped buying bath and body care products. I began using natural products and stopped putting chemicals in my hair. I was becoming a Natural Diva.

And then I revisited a passion from my past: making my own bath and body care products. When we were military and living in Japan, store-bought products were limited. So I created Kym's Heavenly Scents and Gifts to Go. I made things from the heart and put them in baskets to give as gifts. I became known as the "basket lady."

When we returned to the States with all of our stores, I tabled my soap making. But one day after my diagnosis, my husband and I were at a farmers market. We ran across a lady selling soap. That was it. That was my unfinished business. That would be my 2nd Act.

I pulled everything out of my garage – fragrance oils, soap molds, all of it. And I began whipping up products: soaps, lotions, bath salts, scrubs, and shower gels. I realized what I was putting in and on my body was critical to my wellness and cancer. And that was true for others, too.

My friends encouraged me to sell my products. I wanted an updated company name. Basu is a Japanese word for bath. Since the idea had been launched there, it was the perfect. And Branche Basu Boutique was born.

My natural bath and body care products do not harm the skin, maintaining the integrity of our ingredients and our cause: keeping chemicals off other peoples' skin too.

Through the Basu website, I also have the opportunity to create awareness for Multiple Myeloma. I discovered many people had never heard of the disease. And another part of my 2nd act was born.

I partnered with the C.W. Bill Young DoD Marrow Donor Program. They provide medical and logistic support for Department of Defense personnel who want to become donors and save lives.

I held my first bone marrow drive in 2014, with more than 80 potential donors and 12 volunteers for future donor drives.

One of our military members was a match that very first year! It was the best feeling ever. I've held a bone marrow drive every year since, bringing our totals to over 150 potential donors and over 20 volunteers to support the cause.

Having the drive allowed me to share my story with others, and it encouraged others to share their stories, too. Units now host their own bone marrow drives.

I no longer ask myself "why me?" I truly believe God has a reason for everything.

I will never understand it all, but I am truly grateful that he choose me to step into these wonderful 2nd Acts. They have allowed me to walk into a purpose I did not know was there.

I'm still a busy bee, volunteering at my daughter's high school and in other ways. I watched both of my older kids walk across the stage at Grand Canyon University to receive their Bachelor's Degree. And I'm pursing my doctoral degree in Marriage and Family Counseling.

We can never let cancer steal our joy. We must find our passion and use our faith to keep us going.

One of my favorite quotes is by ESPN anchor, Stuart Scott: "You beat cancer by how you live, why you live, and in the manner in which you live."

And I'm living well!

CHAPTER **30:** KIMBERLY BRANCHE

CHAPTER 31

HOLLY ROSE

Breast Cancer Survivor

Holly is a devoted wife and mother of two beautiful girls. Filled with a desire to give back after conquering breast cancer, she founded *Don't be a Chump! Check for a Lump!* The organization empowers women with breast cancer facts, directly assists women with free new wigs and hosts free mammogram events. Learn more about her at *CheckForALump.org.*

CHAPTER **31:** HOLLY ROSE

Nine years ago I had no idea I had a 2nd Act in me. I was a happy homemaker taking my care of my husband and our two daughters.

Then one day I was on Facebook. A girlfriend of mine posted a funny advertisement from the non-profit, "Feel Your Boobies," reminding women to perform a breast self-exam. For whatever crazy reason, it stuck in my head and I did a self-exam that evening.

I discovered a lump that turned out to be breast cancer.

I was very fortunate. In finding my cancer in the early stages, I was able to save my breasts, but more importantly I was able to save my life.

I went through nine months of horrifying treatment. During this time, an amazing community showered my family and me with acts of kindness. We had meals delivered to our house for weeks at a time. People came out of the wood-work to scrub my floors, do my laundry, chauffeured my kids and bring me flowers. I was the recipient of so many acts of kindness that were life-changing for me. And I knew I wanted to do something to give back to my community.

Initially, I thought I would do what someone had done for me: remind other women to do timely breast exams and mammograms to help save lives. I'd become the Phoenix affiliate for Feel Your Boobies.

Excitedly, I put on one of their tee shirts and walked

CHAPTER **31:** HOLLY ROSE

out my of bedroom to show my two daughters, then 9 and 10. Their mouths dropped open and their eyes widened.

"MOM!" they screamed. "You can't wear that!"

I was puzzled. "Why not?"

"Boobies, Mom!"

I thought I'd negotiate a little. "Then can I put a sticker on my car?"

"Absolutely not!" came the response.

I couldn't do anything that would embarrass my daughters. So I found a way to share the same message. And Don't Be a Chump! Check for a Lump! was born. And this is where my 2nd Act really began!

Of course, I had no idea the monstrous test of courage I was about to undertake.

It's funny. During my treatment, all of my friends and family kept telling me how courageous I was, how strong I was. I didn't feel very courageous.

It wasn't like I challenged breast cancer to a duel and said, "Come on, I'll take you on!" My diagnosis came from out of left field. I was 39 with a husband and two daughters.

I didn't have a choice but to accept any and all

treatment offered to me. I had to take it – for them.

But I did have a choice in starting a non-profit on my own. That took courage!

Now you might think my courage is misplaced, but if you had known me nine years ago, you would think differently.

I had been painfully shy my entire life. I experienced social anxiety ever since I was a child and it filled me with fear. Fear of being noticed … fear of rejection … fear of ever having to speak in public. Everyone said I would burst out of my shell. But I never did. As an adult, I still felt like the awkward little redhead with pigtails, freckles and a bad sunburn.

I obviously wasn't a natural born leader, but after my cancer journey, I had a deep passion to give back.

It was almost as if God had spoke to me and said, "Holly, THIS is your purpose in life. Now go. Share with the world."

There have been so many moments of fear that paralyzed me from pursuing this path. But God kept giving me signs that now said, "Holly, pay attention! I already told you! Go! Share!"

Let me tell you, when you think God is speaking to you and then yelling at you . . . well, you listen. This meant I would have to stand up and speak.

CHAPTER **31: HOLLY ROSE**

I would have to ask my entire community to rally around me to get my non-profit up and running. I would have to share my story, my joy, my pain, my tears, EVERYTHING in public!

And so, I dug in deep. I faced my fears and I pushed my boundaries. I looked towards the women in my community who were outspoken and gracious, and who I deeply admired. I observed them: the way they engaged people, their body language and their presence.

Then I practiced modeling them. I walked into a room with a smile, a forced smile, but a smile none the less.

I initiated conversations with women I didn't know. Next, I made the giant leap and I placed myself in front of large crowds of people to share my journey, my passion, my purpose.

I stood trembling before people, my voice quivering, my hands shaking and my legs wobbling. I couldn't help but share my tears too, but I spoke anyway. I was horrible and I was humiliated, but I went right back out there and I did it again and again and again.

My 2nd Act started out as a simple call to action, reminding women to perform breast self-exams and to have timely mammograms.

As I immersed myself in the breast cancer community, I discovered that there were many women going

CHAPTER **31:** HOLLY ROSE

through treatment who were forced to go without a wig simply due to lack of funds. Unfortunately, most insurance companies do not cover the cost of a wig. This was horrifying to me.

Having gone through it all, I can tell you there is absolutely nothing pretty about pink when you are told you have breast cancer. Or when you're told you'll have to go through chemotherapy, lose your hair and be completely bald.

A woman losing her hair is not simply a matter of vanity. It is so much more than that. It is often our identity . . . as a woman, wife, mother, grandmother, sister, daughter, friend. It's everything.

I can attest to this. Losing my hair was one of the most devastating side effects of my chemotherapy. Again, it wasn't vanity. It was the fact that my youngest daughter would not hug me if I wasn't wearing a wig.

It wasn't because she stopped loving me. I just didn't look like mommy any longer. I looked like the face of cancer and I scared her. I was very fortunate. I could walk into a wig shop, pick out a beautiful wig that looked exactly like me, like mommy.

As a result of knowing the emotional devastation caused by losing one's hair we started our extremely innovative wig program to directly assist breast cancer patients. It's different from every other wig program in our state.

CHAPTER **31: HOLLY ROSE**

Not a wig bank, our program gives a woman the privilege of walking into a normal wig shop and selecting any wig of her choice. We pay the bill, up to $250. And then she, too, can look just like herself.

Since our inception we have assisted over 1,000 women with a free wig, and we're now providing wigs to nearly one woman a day.

With support from our community, our non-profit has grown from a tiny grass-roots organization to a prominent figure in the breast cancer community. We now offer a comprehensive education program that is reaching thousands of women and saving lives. We have started, grown and sustained our wig program.

We have been able to initiate a mammogram assistance program to break down financial barriers for women in need. We have provided over 100 free, life-saving mammograms. We have become the go-to for breast cancer in-formation, prevention, and direct assistance in Arizona.

In pursuing my 2nd Act, I found out what courage really meant for me. It meant to be afraid and yet still walk into the darkness. It meant to fall and be utterly humiliated in front of others, and to get back up again not knowing the outcome. It meant to be vulnerable, and be okay with that.

I'm still scared to death, even now after eight years of practice. Yet surprisingly, I'm known for being an

---

CHAPTER **31:** HOLLY ROSE

inspiring speaker, a great speaker! No one would ever know I suffered from shyness. For me, the old adage is really true: "Fake it till you make it."

I stand before you now, still afraid, still with red hair and freckles. But God placed me upon my 2nd Act journey. With HIS help, hard work and an amazing community supporting me, Don't Be a Chump! Check for a Lump! has truly made a difference in the fight against breast cancer.

And I will continue to follow my 2nd Act courageously with all of my heart and soul.

CHAPTER **31:** HOLLY ROSE

CHAPTER **32**

DONNA MOORE
Uterine Adenosarcoma and Breast
Cancer Survivor

Donna started the first 21 years of her life in Georgia, before moving to Portland, OR, and finally to Phoenix. Her passion is for life and time is her most valuable asset: she makes the most of them every day. Since her cancer adventure, she provides support to others as they wade through their own cancer adventures.

CHAPTER **32:** DONNA MOORE

I first learned about cancer at age 12 when my grandfather was diagnosed, and was taken from us within six months. Little did I know how much more I would be impacted by cancer.

Aunts, uncles, clients, friends, my mother, my father, my BFF. And then me. In June, 2010, I was diagnosed with adenosarcoma of the uterus, a very rare and aggressive cancer.

My pathology report started with the words, "This is a very difficult and unusual case," words that shook me to the core.

My treatment would be a complete hysterectomy, followed by inpatient chemotherapy with a 72-hour continual drip. That's right: 72 straight hours, requiring me to be hospitalized for five days every 21 days, for 14 months.

I couldn't believe my ears. Even with all the exposure I had had to cancer, I had never heard of such lengthy treatment. To say I was scared is an understatement. Oh, and one more thing: there are no known survivors with this type of metastatic cancer, anywhere in the world.

This cancer has a very high recurrence rate. It will hide and reappear whenever it feels like it.

But I have reconciled with God. Whatever His will is, I'm okay with. It doesn't mean I don't panic when something seems strange in my body. But I rejoice each time I learn it is not a recurrence of the adenosarcoma.

Panic is exactly what happened in August, 2014 when I found a lump in my breast. It was biopsied and the result was breast cancer. WOOHOO! It's only breast cancer. People thought I was crazy to be happy it was "just breast cancer." After all, I had lost my BFF to breast cancer just two years earlier.

I know it kills. Mine required a bilateral mastectomy and ten years worth of hormone pills. The consensus is that I will have no further issues with breast cancer.

And then there was the large amount of blood in my urine. It turned out to be caused by a kidney stone, easily removed.

WOO HOO again! I have a kidney stone! In both instances, it was the silver lining I had hoped for, as it was not a recurrence of adenosarcoma. It is also how I dealt with my cancer adventure, always looking for the silver lining. I knew there would be one. I just needed to look for it.

Did I mention there are no known survivors of this metastatic cancer? That is until now. And it's me. I am the sole survivor of this metastatic cancer. But I will not be the last.

My oncologists have told me I'm already a miracle, and they're sure I'll be the one to change the statistics.

CHAPTER **32:** DONNA MOORE

I recognize I am different.

So my 2nd Act is very unstructured. I haven't created a foundation, or targeted a select group of people to help. My 2nd Act is conducted in more of a free-spirit way; and somehow, word gets to the people who can benefit from my story. Sometimes it's a neighbor calling to tell me about a friend who has cancer. Would I be willing to talk to them?

Other times our minister asks if I can speak to a congregant with a new cancer diagnosis. And then there's my oncologist, who invites me to do lectures with him to second year medical students. I tell them firsthand about cancer survivorship and the role they will play in that survivorship as doctors.

Sharing with others how I survived a – as my oncologist labels it – "nasty-ass cancer," and not only live, but thrive, that is my 2nd Act. I attribute my survival to so many different things, all of which are now how I live my life.

When treatment was over and I was declared in complete remission, it was time to get back to a normal life. But I'm different now and I intend to be abnormal for the rest of my life. Abnormal from my previous normal.

I feel God has given me a chance to wipe all that out and start over: everything new, everything different, and this time, everything true.

CHAPTER **32:** DONNA MOORE

My relationship with God grew profoundly starting with diagnosis day. I witnessed firsthand how miracles do happen, and how God always gives you what you need when you need it, all in divine order.

I see God in everything now. This is not to say I wear rose-colored glasses, as I know there is pain and suffering in the world. But I feel God is there, especially to those who are willing to open their eyes and see Him.

Our church has a Prayer Chaplain program, which provided me two prayer chaplains through my adventure. They were absolutely a God send for me. They visited me weekly for 14 months, and prayed with me. I was so blessed to have this spiritual support and developed a yearning to pay that forward.

So I am now a Prayer Chaplain at our church, and get the opportunity to pray one-on-one with anyone who needs or wants prayer. Never in my previous life would I have seen this coming.

My oncologist did genetic testing after the discovery of my breast cancer to ascertain my cancer risk. I was guessing pretty high having already had it twice! But he wanted to specifically know what gene mutations I might have and what other cancers might be on the horizon.

The results are I have an ATM mutation (which I got from my Dad who was recently tested), making me at risk for uterine, breast and pancreatic cancer. I've

CHAPTER **32:** DONNA MOORE

had two out of three. My oncologist suggested I enroll in the Early Detection Program at the Virginia Piper Research Center.

The program specifically screens for pancreatic cancer, which is very difficult to diagnose. I am now part of that clinical trial, helping cancer researchers come closer to early detection and potentially a cure.

During my cancer adventure, I sent out regular email updates to family and friends.

I received overwhelming responses, most telling me I should consider writing a book. I took them up on the challenge.

However, when I lost my BFF, I also lost my desire to finish the book. But then, in the last three months, with the encouragement of the most supportive husband in the world, I finished it.

It is in the final editing stage and scheduled to be published in April. My hope is that this book will encourage anyone with a life threatening illness to look at it differently and approach it positively. All profits from my book will go toward programs to do just that.

The book provides the details of different techniques I used to survive. For example, the morning we were leaving for the hospital for my hysterectomy, I wrote "HANDLE WITH LOVE" on my abdomen with a green Sharpie pen.

When I got to the pre-op area, before I let nurses do anything to me, I pulled up my gown and showed them the words on my belly – telling them these were their instructions. It created the icebreaker needed to relax us all. Engaging medical personnel with me on a personal level was paramount to my survival.

I look forward to using the words "HANDLE WITH LOVE" as my life motto. They're the title of my book and the message I want to share with my sister survivors.

CHAPTER **33**

LYNNE HARTKE
Breast Cancer Survivor

Lynne celebrates the difficult and the beautiful with her husband, Kevin, in Chandler, AZ, where they have pastored a church for over 3o years. Lynne writes, volunteers, and keeps up with her four grown children and three grandchildren. Lynne is the author of *Under a Desert Sky: Redefining Hope, Beauty, and Faith in the Hardest Places.* Learn more about her at *LynneHartke. com.*

CHAPTER **33:** LYNNE HARTKE

In my journey from there to here, I never planned to be an author. I was content as a pastor's wife and worship leader at our church, as a mom and a grandma.

Even though I loved books and began my first journal when I was seven years old — a crayon diary of the kittens in the hay mow — I never envisioned myself as an author.

No. Never. Words were my dad's thing.

Dad was a 9th grade English teacher who promised the class each year that if they all got 100% on their weekly spelling tests, he would stand on his head. On his desk. Dad was a bit fanatical about words.

The summer I was 16, I was at a camp for one month. I sent weekly letters home to my parents. On mail day during the third week of camp, I was surprised to receive two letters from home.

I opened Mom's letter first, saving Dad's letter for last – a rare treat to be savored.

Mom's letter was filled with stories of the new baby rabbits in the hutch by the barn, of the green beans almost ready to be picked, and what she was bringing to the potluck at church that Sunday.

Ripping open the second envelope, I was puzzled when I took out the two letters I had sent to them the previous weeks, both neatly corrected by my dad.

CHAPTER **33**: LYNNE HARTKE

The following edits were made in red pen: an added apostrophe, several commas and a note scribbled in his handwriting on when to use "loose" and "lose."

In closing, "Love, Dad" written in the side margin. Like I said, he was fanatical about words and their proper use.

Fast forward to 2009 when I was diagnosed with breast cancer. I remember flipping open my phone to call my husband using slow-motion fingers. When he answered the phone, no words would come out. How was I going to tell him that I had the same disease that killed both his parents? All I could do was sob. Cancer had stolen my words.

I began treatment. The cancer had been caught early. Prognosis was good.

But then my dad was diagnosed with stage 4 melanoma, followed soon afterwards by my mom with stage 3 ovarian which quickly digressed to stage 4.

Suddenly all of us were seeing oncologists and dealing with the editing pen of cancer, slashing with red marks on all of our lives.

For us, cancer became cancel. Cancer your plans. Cancer your dreams. Cancer your life.

After my parents started treatment, I discovered the words that had been silenced from my tongue on the day of my diagnosis, began to bubble up inside me and refused to be silenced.

I began blogging. Writing. Telling our family's story. At first, I would ask Dad and Mom to proofread my posts, because one of my strongest beliefs was, and still is, that people's stories belong to them.

But soon, Dad told me that I didn't need to check with them any longer, that I could write whatever I wanted. What? What did he mean I could write whatever I wanted? What about the proper use of lay and lie and (gasp) dangling prepositions? And what if – heaven forbid — I had an apostrophe out of place?

But then I realized something.

I realized they wanted me to record their story, to give words to their suffering, to inscribe their names onto paper and declare, "We were here." And the seed of a 2nd Act was planted.

One of the greatest gifts we give those who are suffering is to stand with them and announce, "I will be your witness."

Later, when I began talking to those in the publishing industry about writing our family's story, I was told politely, and in no uncertain terms, that with 1.6 million people diagnosed with cancer each year, I was not famous enough to represent the cancer community.

Another red pen.

CHAPTER **33:** LYNNE HARTKE

I will spare you the long details, but in May, 2017, God chose to swing wide the door of our family's story when my book was traditionally published with the title, *Under a Desert Sky: Redefining Hope, Beauty and Faith in the Hardest Places.*

Cancer could not silence the words.

And now I teach a workshop to other cancer survivors, helping them record their words. I have taught survivors from stage 1 to stage 4, those who are newly diagnosed and those who have been survivors for many years. I have stood as a witness to their brave stories.

Perhaps, you have known the red pen of cancer; the editing voice inside your head that tells you that your story is not valuable.

It is a lie.

Give words to your story. There are 1.6 million people diagnosed with cancer each year. We don't need fewer stories, we need more.

Survivor stories are the foundation of the organization A 2nd Act, as well as being the foundation of my own 2nd Act.

You see, I discovered my dad was right. There is an important difference between "loose" and "lose." Of all the things the red pen of cancer has taken, please

---

CHAPTER **33:** LYNNE HARTKE

don't LOSE your story. Don't ever allow cancer to erase your words.